wheel to wheel

wheel to wheel

The Great Duels of Formula One Racing

Alan Henry

PHOENIX ILLUSTRATED

contents

introduction   **6**

1 | **fangio** and **moss**
                          rivalry and affection   **12**

2 | **clark** and **hill**
                          the gentleman racers   **24**

3 | **stewart** and **rindt**
                          friendship and respect   **36**

4 | **lauda** and **hunt**
                          opposites attract   **46**

6 **prost** and **lauda**

new stars for old   **70**

7 **mansell** and **piquet**

poles apart   **82**

8 **prost** and **senna**

world war III   **94**

9 **hill** and **schumacher**

magnetic attraction   **106**

10 **villeneuve** and **schumacher**

head to head   **120**

introduction

Wheel to wheel. Three words which utterly encompass the unique environment of front-line Grand Prix motor racing. Some commentators believe it to be the ultimate sporting spectacle, others simply warfare waged with automobiles. Ever since motor racing began, there have been particular, dramatic rivalries to capture the spectators' imagination.

This book deals with some of the great confrontations between the most gifted drivers of their eras. In essence, it also tracks the manner in which Grand Prix racing has subtly evolved over the four and a half decades since the official World Championship contest was inaugurated in 1950. It takes the story from the intensely professional relationship between Stirling Moss and Juan Manuel Fangio at a time when motor racing had a strictly defined etiquette which top drivers strayed from at their peril, through to the unruly, high-profile, televized battles between Damon Hill and Michael Schumacher in the mid-1990s.

The factors which throw individual drivers into an unusually tense, polarized contest, with either a rival from another team or an ostensible running mate driving the same car, are many and varied. For

Previous page: Explosive quartet. Left to right, Ayrton Senna, Alain Prost, Nigel Mansell and Nelson Piquet before the 1986 Australian GP. All would tangle with each other during their distinguished careers.

Left: Start of the 1984 Portuguese GP, with Keke Rosberg in the lead. The race was won by Alain Prost, but Niki Lauda took the championship by half a point!

Did he throw the race? The legendary Fangio during the 1955 British GP. Stirling Moss won that day, but will never know whether the maestro permitted him to do so.

Playing it by the book. Jochen Rindt's Lotus leads his close friend Jackie Stewart's Matra during their flawless battle for the lead of the 1969 British GP.

example, Enzo Ferrari was an autocratic patriarch who ran his team with a rod of iron and liked nothing more than pitching his own drivers into simmering cauldrons of internecine strife, revelling in the sight of his own cars racing amongst themselves as much as against the opposition.

In this connection, the period between 1956 and 1958 was particularly lurid, with Italians Luigi Musso and Eugenio Castellotti ranged successively against Fangio and British drivers Mike Hawthorn and Peter Collins.

The tensions ran wildly out of control as Ferrari was always reluctant to nominate a specific team leader. The pressure would eventually cause Castellotti to be killed testing at Modena and Musso and Collins to die at the height of racing action, respectively in the 1958 French and German Grands Prix. As a final ironic twist, Hawthorn was killed in a road accident near Guildford, southern England, in January 1959, a matter of weeks after announcing his retirement from racing.

Ferrari's unwillingness to control its drivers survived into the 1980s, when Gilles Villeneuve and

Didier Pironi picked up the threads of this highly political cut-and-thrust. By the same token, Frank Williams liked nothing better than watching as his own Formula 1 cars raced each other into the ground, as witness the battles between Nigel Mansell and Nelson Piquet in the mid-1980s, which are dealt with in Chapter Seven.

Later still, McLaren boss Ron Dennis tacitly acquiesced in the intra-team battles between Ayrton Senna and Alain Prost during the 1988 and 1989 Grand Prix seasons. At the end of the day, though, Senna's ruthlessness would drive Prost from the team at the end of the latter season, despite huge efforts on the part of Dennis to retain the brilliant Frenchman's services. But, as you will see in Chapter Eight, that parting of the ways was by no means the end of the Prost/Senna story.

The Damon Hill/Michael Schumacher saga is the most recent chapter of frenzied rivalry on the Grand Prix stage. Where it will end is anybody's guess. The only thing certain is that it isn't the first such confrontation and most certainly will not be the last.

Close call. Damon Hill's Williams locks a brake as the Englishman challenges Michael Schumacher's Benetton early in the 1994 Australian GP at Adelaide. Later, the confrontation would end in tears.

fangio and moss

rivalry and affection

An extraordinary relationship of mutual trust, respect and affection grew up in 1955 between Juan Manuel Fangio and Stirling Moss when they were paired together in the factory Mercedes-Benz team for the German company's first post-war assault on the Grand Prix winner's circle.

Right: Battling against the odds. Fangio's Maserati (No 2, far right) accelerating away from the start of the 1957 Italian Grand Prix alongside the Vanwalls driven by Stuart Lewis-Evans, Stirling Moss and Tony Brooks.

Fangio already had two World Championships to his credit at the age of 44, while Moss was only 25 and in his first full Formula 1 season with a works team. Yet in those days the conventions of respect and consideration had not been swept from the Grand Prix stage by the win-at-all-costs ethos which lured Formula 1 into such stormy waters a generation or more later. Sure enough, the aim was to win, but also to play by the book.

Fangio came from a humble background in provincial Argentina and never lost sight of his roots as he climbed the ladder of international racing success. His father had been an immigrant Italian who worked variously as a plasterer and potato farmer. The young Juan had worked in a garage during his youth and almost succumbed to pneumonia before making his racing reputation in the gruelling road races which criss-crossed South America in the immediate post-war years.

Fangio came to Europe for an exploratory visit in 1948 and returned the following year for a full programme of Formula 1 races at the wheel of a Maserati financed by the Argentinian government. He immediately displayed winning form and duly accepted an invitation to drive for the works Alfa Romeo team the following year – the equivalent of a first-year novice today being invited to join Benetton or Williams with only a handful of races under his belt.

In 1951 Fangio won his first World Championship title for Alfa Romeo and, after a difficult couple of seasons with Maserati, was signed by Mercedes-Benz to spearhead their Grand Prix comeback in 1954 and 1955. The revived German team was planning to make its debut sometime during the course of the 1954 season and, in the meantime, Fangio was released to drive for Maserati until Mercedes was ready to start.

Fangio leads Moss in the British Grand Prix at Aintree, where Moss turned the tables and won. Or did he?

Previous page: The pupil and the master. Moss and Fangio share the laurel wreaths at the end of the 1955 British Grand Prix.

Fangio after winning his final Grand Prix at Nurburgring in 1957, when his Maserati trounced the Ferraris of Peter Collins (left) and Mike Hawthorn. Like Moss, these two other Englishmen revered the ace from Argentina.

Meanwhile, unbeknown to either of them, the professional racing careers of Fangio and a young Englishman were converging. Stirling Moss was the son of a prosperous and successful dentist who had raced as an amateur at Indianapolis in the 1920s. Stirling and his sister Pat were raised in a highly competitive, sport-orientated environment and, before cars came into their lives, both established a reputation as top-class show jumpers.

In 1948, when Fangio was making his first visit to Europe, Stirling had hurled himself into the turbulently competitive world of 500cc Formula 3 racing. He quickly established himself as the dominant force in the cut-and-thrust of this category right through to 1954, when he finally gave it up on the eve of his graduation to front-line Formula 1 at the wheel of a Maserati 250F.

In 1951 Moss was given the chance to race internationally by the struggling HWM team, but their finances were as brittle as the cars they built and no success came his way. Then, at the end of 1953, the racing world snapped to attention with the news that Mercedes would be returning to F1 the following year. Together with Stirling's manager Ken Gregory, Alfred Moss approached Mercedes team manager Alfred Neubauer with the suggestion that his son might be considered for a place in the line-up alongside Fangio.

Neubauer was interested in the idea, knowing full well of young Stirling's potential. But he did not feel that Mercedes could risk fielding a driver who had no proven experience in a competitive Grand Prix car. However, the Mercedes manager did not close the door. In effect, he told Stirling's father: "Get him a drive in a decent F1 car; let's see what he can do – and come back and talk again next year."

Alfred Moss and Gregory then persuaded British Petroleum to help finance the purchase of a private Maserati 250F for young Stirling to use in 1954. The 250F was one of the all-time classic Grand Prix cars; a fine-handling and forgiving machine which, in contemporary parlance, could be considered 'user friendly' if not always absolutely the most competitive machine available.

It did the trick for Stirling Moss. Although he failed to win a single Grand Prix in 1954, the brilliant young Englishman dominated the Italian race at Monza, his private Maserati pulling away from Fangio's Mercedes before retiring with loss of oil pressure. Alfred Neubauer was now totally convinced and an invitation for Stirling to join the Mercedes-Benz team in 1955 was soon forthcoming.

Fangio's efforts at the wheel of a Maserati and Mercedes had enabled him to clinch the 1954 World Championship – his second – and he was absolutely determined to win his third in 1955. The season opened on Fangio's home turf in Buenos Aires, where he dominated the Argentine Grand Prix in sweltering conditions, with Moss coming home fourth, sharing another Mercedes W196 with team-mates Hans Herrmann and Karl Kling after his own original car stopped on the circuit with fuel vapour lock.

The image of Mercedes-Benz as a supremely dominant Grand Prix operation has been lovingly burnished over the years by fans of the three-pointed star. Yet the truth of the matter is that the Mercedes W196 was only an adequately reliable machine, its achievements flattered by lack of strong opposition.

Both Fangio and Moss suffered engine failures in the second race at Monaco, and although they bounced back to finish first and second in the Belgian Grand Prix at Spa, there was no doubt that the striking new Lancia D50 more than had their measure in terms of out-and-out competitiveness.

Sadly, the death of the legendary Alberto Ascari, Lancia's number one driver, whilst testing a sports Ferrari at Monza barely a week after escaping unhurt when he crashed into the harbour at Monaco, was the final straw for the Italian team. The cash-strapped Gianni Lancia withdrew from racing and

these technically exquisite cars were handed over to Ferrari, who bastardized them into the role of also-ran over the next couple of seasons.

Fangio and Moss then finished first and second ahead of Luigi Musso in the Dutch Grand Prix at Zandvoort before heading for Liverpool's Aintree circuit and the British Grand Prix.

This race represented a potentially delicate public relations operation for Mercedes-Benz. Only ten years had passed since the end of the Second World War and the average Englishman was still pretty ambivalent towards the Germans as a nation. Inflamed passions lurked below the surface of apparently straight-laced emotions. Tactfully, for this race, Stirling's silver Mercedes carried a Union Jack sticker prominently on its tail fairing. But there was an even more conciliatory gesture to come.

This was the first post-war British Grand Prix not to be held at Silverstone. The previous year, for the race on the former aerodrome track, Mercedes had fielded its W196 challengers fitted with full-width

Fangio on his way to victory in the German Grand Prix in 1957.

aerodynamic bodywork and had been taken to the cleaners by Fangio's compatriot Froilan Gonzalez at the wheel of a Ferrari. Now, against the backdrop of the Grand National horse-racing course, the German team was hoping for better things.

Getting on terms with Mercedes, let alone beating the 'Silver Arrows', was clearly going to be a task well beyond any of the opposition at Aintree that weekend. Moss just managed to pip Fangio for pole position and only the gallant Jean Behra's efforts in his scarlet works Maserati 250F, third fastest, upset the symmetry of the front row. On the second row sat the other two Mercedes, driven by Germany's Karl Kling and the Italian veteran Piero Taruffi.

At the start, Fangio eased seamlessly into an immediate lead, but let Moss by without any fuss after only three laps. Thereafter, the two Mercedes W196 simply streaked away into the distance, Behra's last vestige of opposition vanishing after only ten laps when his Maserati's hard-worked engine failed terminally and spectacularly.

On lap 17, Fangio retook the lead, but allowed Moss back ahead after only another nine laps. All eyes were now firmly watching the silver Mercedes with the Union Jack transfer on its tail. Just how would this fascinating contest be resolved?

Fangio knew that his third World Championship was in the bag, irrespective of the outcome of this particular race. The public relations benefits of allowing Moss to win at Aintree would be immeasurable. Stirling was then very much the 'Golden Boy' of the British sporting world; the dazzling young talent who was making his mark on the international stage. What had Fangio to lose?

On the face of it, all Stirling had to do was to keep out of trouble. Yet the pressure on him was considerable. Here he was in the best car in the business, still a long way to go to the finish and a twice World Champion tracking his progress, marking his every move. The unspoken question in everybody's mind was crystal clear: was Fangio sandbagging to make the young Englishman look good?

With ten laps left to run, Moss seemed to have his first Grand Prix victory in the palm of his hand. He had eased open a four-second advantage over Fangio, yet as the final laps ticked away, the

Left: Fangio at Nurburgring in 1956 during the German Grand Prix, at the height of a hard season for Ferrari.

Luigi Mosso, seen here in his Ferrari 801 in the 1957 French Grand Prix, had been one of Fangio's team-mates the previous year. Unlike Moss at Mercedes, he was a less willing pupil and might have enjoyed more success had he paid heed to Fangio's advice.

Fangio leads Moss in a Mercedes 1-2 at the Dutch Grand Prix in 1955.

Right and below: Moss in the Vanwall challenges and overtakes Fangio's Maserati. in the five-times champion's final race, the 1958 French Grand Prix at Reims.

Argentine ace came shimmering up behind him once again. Going into the final lap, the two Mercedes were running absolutely nose-to-tail.

The tension was unbearable as all eyes in the start/finish grandstand strained to pick out the two silver dots as they streaked down Railway Straight for the last time. Through the tricky Melling Crossing, where the race track crossed the horse-racing course, and suddenly they were back, braking hard for the final right-hand Tatts Corner.

Moss was still ahead, but as the two Mercedes accelerated hard for the line, Fangio drew almost level. As they took the chequered flag, his front wheels were level with Stirling's cockpit. But the 26-year-old Englishman had at last won his maiden Grand Prix victory. Moss was almost overcome by emotion, placing his winner's laurels round Fangio's shoulders as they celebrated their joint success.

At the end of the 1955 season, Mercedes-Benz withdrew from Grand Prix racing. Moss and Fangio went their separate ways to continue their F1 careers; Stirling back to Maserati, now as a works driver, Fangio to Ferrari for a difficult run to his fourth World Championship title.

Moss then switched to Tony Vandervell's Vanwall team in 1957, realising a long-held ambition to drive for a competitive British team. Fangio returned to his first love, Maserati, and rounded off his career with a fifth World Championship. Mid way through 1958 he decided that it was time to stop and he retired to Buenos Aires and his prosperous business as Argentina's Mercedes-Benz importer.

Moss raced on to win a total of 16 Grands Prix, but never a World Championship, before retiring from the cockpit after a dreadful accident at Goodwood on Easter Monday 1962 which left him in a coma and partly paralysed for many weeks. Yet

both men would continue to play a prominent role as members of the international motor-racing community; Moss, the effervescently energetic youngster who never seemed to age, Fangio the increasingly revered Father Figure whose presence in the Grand Prix pit lane during his later years was akin to the arrival of royalty.

In the late 1980s, despite now being elderly and infirm, Fangio took a great interest in the career of the brilliant Brazilian driver Ayrton Senna. There was more than half a century separating their ages, but Fangio had an instinctive regard for the younger man, perhaps recognising in him all the competitive motivation which had originally fired his own professional career back in the late 1940s. When Senna won the 1991 Brazilian Grand Prix at Interlagos – his first such home win – he invited Fangio to join him on the rostrum. Like Moss more than thirty years earlier, Senna deeply admired Fangio's greatness, both as a driver and as a man.

> If Fangio did slip Moss the win, it was a move delivered with such strategic subtlety and style that nobody can be quite sure to this day.

For his part, to this day Stirling Moss is not quite sure what really happened at Aintree on that July afternoon over forty years ago. "I asked Fangio many times about it," he reflects. "I know I was driving well that day, but, boy, the Old Man seemed to be able to pull up alongside me any time he liked." Fangio would always shrug the question aside: "No, no, he beat me. He had a lower final drive ratio fitted to his car before the race and there was no way my car could catch his on acceleration."

If Fangio did slip Moss the win, it was a move delivered with such strategic subtlety and style that nobody will ever be quite sure. Fangio died in July 1995, mourned as one by the entire motor-racing world. The secret went with him to his grave, leaving Stirling Moss in the very forefront of those colleagues who loved and admired his understated greatness as a professional sportsman.

Moss's career continued onwards and upwards in the post-Fangio era. Here at Reims, a year after Fangio's last race at the same circuit, Stirling's light green BRM P25 is fifth behind Tony Brooke's winning Ferrari (24), Jack Brabham's Cooper (8), Phil Hill's Ferrari (26) and Bruce McLaren's Cooper.

2 clark and hill

the gentlemen racers

In 1965, Jim Clark missed the Monaco Grand Prix in order to compete in America's famous motor race, the Indianapolis 500. Clark duly won the US classic at the wheel of his Lotus-Ford, leaving his F1 rival Graham Hill to clinch his hat trick of victories through the streets of the Mediterranean Principality. "A shame Jim wasn't there to see it," remarked Hill after this latest meeting with the Rainiers. It was not only a remark typical of Graham's dry humour, but also an accurate barometer of the personal relationship which existed between these two men, who became the leading exponents of the 1.5-litre Grand Prix era which lasted from 1961 to 1965.

Hill's BRM leads Clark's Lotus and Richie Ginther's Honda at the start of the 1965 United States GP.

Right: Graham Hill put BRM on the F1 map with his gritty performances in their 1.5-litre V8 engined cars. Here he is about to win the 1965 United States GP.

Previous page: Jim Clark winning his final Grand Prix in South Africa in 1968.

Graham Hill, born in 1929, was the elder of the dynamic duo by seven years. He came up the hard way, sampling a racing car for the first time in 1953 when he paid a pound for four laps of Brands Hatch in a 500cc Formula 3 car. Hill's other great passion was rowing; he would carry the distinctive vertical white stripes of the London Rowing Club on his helmet throughout his career, as would his son Damon a generation later.

By a process of judicious socializing and hard graft, Graham struck up a relationship with Lotus boss Colin Chapman, got his shoulder to the motor-racing door and eventually made his Grand Prix debut at the wheel of a Lotus at Monaco in 1958. However, in 1960 the moustached Londoner switched to drive for rivals BRM, the team with which he would become most closely identified.

Clark was the unobtrusive, almost shy son of a Scottish border farmer. The family was comfortably fixed, if not exactly wealthy, but Jim's parents would have preferred it had he stuck to farming and were not particularly keen on his motor-racing activities. Jimmy initially raced for Border Reivers, a private team of Scottish enthusiasts, but when one

of their number, Ian Scott-Watson, bought one of the new Lotus Elites and entered it for Clark at the prestigious Boxing Day Brands Hatch meeting at the end of 1958, the blue touch paper was lit and Jimmy's career took off.

In 1960, Clark joined the Team Lotus Formula Junior team and quickly mastered this nursery of future F1 talent. The Scot had originally been contracted to drive in Grands Prix for the Aston Martin team, but this programme was already fading fast before Jim took a turn at the wheel. Eventually Colin Chapman invited him to drive a works Lotus in the Dutch Grand Prix, where he ran fourth before the gearbox seized. The race was won by Jack Brabham's Cooper from the Lotus of Innes Ireland and Graham Hill's BRM.

Neither Clark nor Hill would win races in 1960 or 1961, but the following year their competitive rivalry really got into top gear. Both had new V8 engines from Coventry-Climax and BRM respectively, but Clark had a car advantage in the form of the sensationally sleek Lotus 25 with its revolutionary monocoque chassis. Yet it was Hill who took first blood, winning the opening Grand Prix of the season in the Netherlands after Clark's Lotus wilted on his race debut.

However, once Jim got into his stride, there was no stopping him. He won the Belgian, French and British Grands Prix. Then Hill bounced back to win in Germany and Italy. Clark took the US race at Watkins Glen, comfortably outpacing Hill's BRM, so the destiny of the World Championship would be

Casual chic; Jim Clark, dressed for comfort rather than style with a button-up cardigan atop his overalls, on the startline at the 1965 US Grand Prix.

decided in the last race of the season, the South African Grand Prix at East London.

The BRM team had been under enormous pressure in 1962. The British Racing Motor had been conceived in the immediate post-war years as a national racing-car project, receiving financial support from a wide variety of the country's industrialists. The project was eventually taken over by leading industrialist Sir Alfred Owen's Rubery Owen group, but BRM was dogged by lack of success throughout the 1950s and arrived on the verge of

the 1962 season with only a single Grand Prix win to its credit.

Owen made it plain; win at least two Grands Prix in 1962, or the team will be closed down. Thanks to Hill's dependability and determination, BRM held the line and survived. Now, going into the East London race, Hill had taken BRM to the very edge of a World Championship title.

It was a two-horse race. Clark qualified on pole ahead of the BRM star and quickly pulled away into an early lead. Soon the Scot was out on his own in

Clark at his brilliant best, winning the 1967 Dutch GP at Zandvoort on the debut outing of the sensational Lotus-Ford 49.

Graham Hill leads commandingly for Lotus in the opening phase of the 1967 Dutch Grand Prix.

the Lotus 25, nursing a half-minute lead and heading for his own first championship crown.

Then, almost imperceptibly, Clark's Lotus began to trail a thin haze of oil. Hill suddenly made up two seconds. Before long, Jimmy came hurtling into the pits. The engine cover was ripped off, but the oil leak could not be quenched. He was out of the race, leaving Graham to surge through to win BRM's sole World Championship. It was a seminal moment in post-war Formula 1 history.

Clark would more than make up for this disappointment in 1963, when a driver's best six results were permitted to count for the championship. He won the Belgian, Dutch, French, British, Mexican and South African races to clinch his first title and leave Hill with only two wins, at Monaco and in North America, as consolation.

A distinct pattern was now emerging. Clark's finger-tip genius meant that, all things being equal, he was more likely than not to beat the dogged, self-

taught Hill in a straight fight. In particular, Clark's genius was put on very public display in torrential rain at Spa Francorchamps in 1963 when he lapped the entire field on this eight-mile circuit, only easing off sufficiently in the closing stages to allow second-place Bruce McLaren's Cooper back on to the same lap before the end.

Clark was also often a lucky driver. In 1964, he would win at Spa yet again, but only after Dan Gurney's Brabham, Hill's BRM and McLaren's Cooper all hit trouble ahead of him in the closing stages of the race. Yet he would be deprived of the 1964 World Championship on the last lap of the final race of the season, in Mexico City, when his Lotus ground to a halt with engine failure.

Mathematically, this should have allowed Graham to take his second championship, but he had been pushed off the road early in the race by Lorenzo Bandini's Ferrari and been forced to come into the pits for repairs to his BRM.

Even so, he was still ahead on points when Clark retired, but quick thinking by the Ferrari team saw them slow Bandini and allow John Surtees through into second place behind Dan Gurney's winning Brabham on the very last lap, thus giving the former motorcycle ace the crown by a single point. This was particularly frustrating for Graham, who had scored a total of 41 points during the course of the year – one more than Surtees's tally – but was only allowed to count 39 of them when the best six results were taken into account!

By now the Grand Prix scene of the 1960s had settled into a comfortable pattern. Clark and Hill were not only established as the two leading F1 exponents of the time, but they also led lives which the average man in the street could identify with. The jet-setting, multi-millionaire tax exiles of the 1990s were still a long way off.

Graham, his wife Bette and their three children, Damon, Brigitte and Samantha, lived comfortably, if unostentatiously, in the north London surburb of Mill Hill. Jimmy, meanwhile, headed back to the family farm, Edington Mains, at Chirnside, near Berwick-upon-Tweed, as often as he could. As the years passed, the young Scot became more cosmopolitan and international in outlook, but his heart remained in his homeland.

In 1965, Clark again took the championship contest by the throat, winning six races to clinch his second crown by the German Grand Prix in August – with three races still left on the calendar. But Formula 1 was destined to be changed fundamentally by the introduction of new 3-litre engine regulations from the start of the 1966 season.

Ford announced plans to become involved in Formula 1 with a major investment in a brand new, state-of-the-art 3-litre Grand Prix engine designed and manufactured by British specialists Cosworth Engineering. This would be ready for 1967 and supplied to Team Lotus on an exclusive basis, initially at least.

The 1966 season proved to be a year of transition. Veteran Aussie Jack Brabham won the World Championship – his third – with a car bearing his own name and powered by an uncomplicated Repco V8 engine based on a Chrysler production unit. Lotus and BRM struggled along, both sharing the latter's complicated and unreliable H-16 cylinder engine. Yet it was ironic that Clark's golden touch should reward him with his sole win of the season in the US Grand Prix – using an engine borrowed from the BRM team the night before the race!

It was at the end of 1966 that Graham Hill decided on a momentous course of action. He had concluded that he was too much part of the furniture at BRM. "I got the impression that it wouldn't be long before I was sprayed dark green and stood in a corner of the team's workshop throughout the off-season," he remarked dryly.

With the new Cosworth Ford DFV engine almost ready to race, Ford wanted Lotus to have two superstar drivers for 1967. So they bankrolled Hill's switch to the team alongside Clark, his longtime rival.

From a distance of thirty years it is almost impossible to convey the shock waves that rippled through the sport when Hill's move to Lotus was made public. In contemporary terms, it was the equivalent of Ferrari announcing that Damon Hill would drive alongside Michael Schumacher for the 1996 season. But without the personal edge or venom, of course.

Clark regarded the deal with the equanimity of a man who rightly believed he could beat his incoming colleague. However, there were subtle signs that he regarded this move as some sort of infringement on his personal status. When asked innocently by a press man how he viewed the prospect of being Graham Hill's team-mate, he replied coolly: "I am not Graham Hill's team-mate. He is my team-mate."

Either way, there was no doubt that the new Lotus 49 was the class of the field in 1967, fundamentally redefining what was required of a competitive Grand Prix car. Hill qualified easily on pole position for the new machine's debut in the Dutch Grand Prix at Zandvoort with Clark coming

> With the new Cosworth Ford DFV engine almost ready to race, Ford wanted Lotus to have two superstar drivers.

Over to the enemy. Hill made the switch to Lotus at the start of 1967 and qualified the new Lotus 49 on pole position for its first race at Zandvoort.

through to score a first-time win after Graham's machine wilted with mechanical problems.

This set the tone for the rest of the year. Hill had the bad luck, Clark all the breaks. Graham looked on course for wins at Silverstone, Monza and Watkins Glen, only to be side-lined each time by mechanical failures.

Then came disaster. On 7 April, 1968, Jim Clark crashed to his death in a minor-league Formula 2 race at Hockenheim, near Heidelberg, sliding off the rain-soaked circuit into the unprotected trees which then lined the track.

Clark won four races, Hill none. But at the end of the season the World Championship went to the consistent Denny Hulme at the wheel of a Brabham-Repco, with only two wins to his credit.

The 1968 season opened with Clark scoring a commanding victory from Hill in the South African Grand Prix. It was the

25th triumph of his career, at last beating Fangio's record of 24 wins, which had remained intact since the great Argentine driver's German Grand Prix win ten years earlier.

Then came disaster. On 7 April, 1968, Jim Clark crashed to his death in a minor-league Formula 2 race at Hockenheim, near Heidelberg, sliding off the rain-soaked circuit into the unprotected trees which then lined the track. It was front-page news across the world. The motor-racing community trembled; Jimmy was regarded as inviolate. If he could be killed, then nobody was safe.

Lotus boss Colin Chapman was consumed by grief. Briefly, he toyed with retiring from the sport. But he decided to continue and Graham Hill would

be the rock on which Lotus leaned heavily to rebuild its efforts and steady its nerve. The Londoner gave Lotus a psychologically crucial victory in the next event, the Spanish Grand Prix at Madrid's Jarama circuit. And he followed that up with the fourth win of his career through the streets of Monaco.

By the end of the season, Hill had successfully clinched his second World Championship title and restored Team Lotus's faith in itself. But somehow, it would never quite be the same for Chapman's team now that Clark was no longer around.

Into 1969 and Hill would win at Monaco for a fifth time. But he was now 40 and, in Chapman's view, already past his peak. Graham was finally

dropped from the team after breaking both legs in a terrible accident during that year's United States Grand Prix and he began a gentle decline, although he would not finally retire from the cockpit until the summer of 1975.

By then he was looking forward to establishing his own fledgeling racing team in the F1 front-line, but in November 1975 he was killed, together with his young star driver Tony Brise and four other team members, when his Piper Aztec aeroplane crashed on Arkley golf course whilst trying to land in foggy conditions at Elstree.

Seven years after the loss of Jim Clark, the motor-racing community mourned again. It was the end of an era.

Hill, soon to assume Lotus team leadership, coming home second at the 1968 South African Grand Prix.

Left: Clark clinched the 1965 World Championship with a flag-to-flag victory in the German Grand Prix. The orange nose of Graham Hill's second-place BRM can be seen leading the pursuit in the distance.

3 stewart and rindt

friendship
and respect

If Jim Clark and Graham Hill somehow evoked memories of the flat-capped, tweed-jacketed image of the motor-racing sportsman, the Swinging Sixties would be encapsulated by their two immediate successors in the Formula 1 front-line, Jackie Stewart and Jochen Rindt. They could hardly have come from more contrasting backgrounds. Yet these two young stars would become genuinely close friends, unyielding competitors who, paradoxically, looked after each other in high-speed wheel-to-wheel battles in an era when erratic indiscipline or questionable driving manoeuvres could have fatal consequences.

Jackie Stewart on his way to victory in the 1970 Whit Monday Crystal Palace F2 international race, driving a Brabham-Cosworth entered by Guildford garage owner John Coombs.

Previous page: Stewart's Matra leads Rindt's Lotus during their battle for the lead of the 1969 Italian Grand Prix at Monza. Stewart beat Rindt by less than a length to clinch his first World Championship.

Jackie Stewart was the dyslexic son of a garage owner from Dumbarton, Scotland, Jochen Rindt the Austrian-raised heir to a German fortune whose parents had been killed in an Allied bombing raid on Hamburg when he was still a baby. They both fought their way up through the minor-league formulae with great distinction before becoming Grand Prix rivals in 1965.

Rindt was born into comfortable financial circumstances, inheriting a share in the Mainz-based spice importers, Klein & Rindt. In his youth he was spoiled by his doting grandparents and he grew into a wilful youngster who got up to some nerve-wracking exploits on skis and sledges even before he was old enough to begin driving at the wheel of an elderly, inherited Volkswagen.

"I was always in trouble at school," reflected Jochen a couple of years before his death. "This was partly because I didn't work very hard and partly because I was always fighting. On one occasion, I almost ran down one of the teachers on my motorcycle, so in the end I got thrown out and went to England to learn English, but I spent most of my time sailing. I was staying not far from Goodwood and, one Sunday, I went to a club race meeting. It looked marvellous!"

Stewart had a more spartan upbringing. His family was comfortably off, but Jackie cut his teeth in his father's garage, working on the petrol pumps and cleaning the floor in the service bay. In many ways he was the caricature of the Scot who knew the price of a dollar. Much later, as a multi-millionaire, he would join in the laughter when Stuart Turner, Ford's competitions boss and a man who assisted his career, told a joke which has become a classic amongst the motor-racing fraternity; "Jackie was arrested last week for breaking into a five pound note – but he was let off with a caution since it was a first offence!"

For British fans it was on 17 May 1964 that Jochen Rindt sprang to international prominence. At the delightful Crystal Palace circuit in south London, Rindt really put his name on the map driving his own Formula 2 Brabham-Cosworth to victory in the 40-lap London Trophy race. Difficult though it may be to believe now, more than 30 years later, but the local newspaper credited Rindt with Australian nationality when reporting his success, presumably on the somewhat xenophobic principle that real racing drivers only came from Britain or its Commonwealth.

Stewart, who had been an accomplished trap shooter before turning his hand to motor racing, was by this time well established on the UK domestic motor-racing scene. He had marked himself out as a man to watch in 1963 with some superb performances driving for the Edinburgh-based Ecurie Ecosse, gaining promotion to Ken Tyrrell's Formula 3 team for 1964 and completely dominating the British championship.

Jackie Stewart recalls meeting Jochen for the first time at Reims in 1964. At the time Jackie and his wife Helen were driving round Europe in their Mini, Jackie contesting various prestige F3 races with the Tyrrell Cooper-BMC squad. Jochen drove an E-type Jaguar and seemed very racy and assured compared with the Scot who, by his own admission, was still wet behind the ears.

"Jochen was fundamentally more polished and worldly than I was," recalls Jackie. Over the next two or three years they would grow to F1 maturity together, sharing the bond that so often springs up between contemporaries in any pursuit.

"In relative terms we were the kids, the new boys," says Jackie. "Jim Clark, Graham Hill, John Surtees and Lorenzo Bandini – they were the big stars. We also looked up to Jo Bonnier as the super-international sophisticate. We were just a couple of

The massed grid before the start at Crystal Palace, 1970. From left to right on the front row, Clay Regazzoni, Jochen Rindt and Jackie Stewart.

In the early stages at Crystal Palace in 1970, with Rindt's Lotus leading Regazzoni's Tecno and Stewart's Brabham-Cosworth.

youngsters, sharing hotel rooms and meals, even going to a drive-in movie together on one occasion, when the South African Grand Prix was held at East London in 1965. I mean, can you imagine that? We were really not very sophisticated at all!"

Jochen drove his first Formula 1 race in the 1964 Austrian Grand Prix on the bumpy Zeltweg aerodrome circuit at the wheel of a Brabham-BRM fielded by British private owner Rob Walker, scion

of the Johnny Walker whisky dynasty. The following season, Rindt signed a three-year deal to drive for the works Cooper team, which was by then at the start of a gentle decline. Stewart, more shrewdly perhaps, joined the front-running BRM team as partner to Graham Hill, father of current Williams driver Damon.

In 1965, Jochen had a difficult freshman year in Formula 1. The Cooper was frankly uncompetitive

and he seldom saw much of Jackie on the circuit. His best placing was a determined fourth in the German Grand Prix – his adopted home event – at the Nurburgring. Stewart, by contrast, had a run of splendid second places to Jim Clark's Lotus and then crowned his first F1 year with victory in the Italian Grand Prix at Monza.

It would not be long before the Rindt and Stewart families would be living a short distance apart on the shores of Lake Geneva, tax exiles both. Jochen was married to the striking Finnish model Nina Lincoln. As Stewart remembers: " It was a turbulent relationship all the way to the end. Nina was a total-ly independent girl with independent means and had enjoyed a very successful modelling career in Paris, New York and Milan. Her father also looked after her very well. She knew what she wanted and where she wanted to go. They used to have awful arguments, something I would never have thought of having so publicly with Helen, for example. But it was a very different mood. It was very chauvinistic in Scotland at that time. I mean, you got married and your wife didn't work. I thought Jochen and Nina were very Continental!"

Stewart wound up third in the 1965 championship, then seventh, ninth and second respectively over the next three years before taking the first of his three titles in 1969. By the start of 1969 he had

> Jackie Stewart and Jochen Rindt were now more closely matched than at any time previously in their careers, going out to do battle at Silverstone armed with the Ford Cosworth-powered Matra MS80 and Lotus 49B respectively.

already won five Grands Prix, while Rindt, who followed three bleak years at Cooper with an equally unproductive partnership with Brabham in 1968, had still to win his first.

Yet consistent success in Formula 2, where the cars and engines were much more closely matched than in F1, ensured that Rindt's reputation continued to be surrounded with relish and anticipation. He had the speed and the skill. Now all he needed was the car.

Finally, in 1969, he joined Lotus and that year's British Grand Prix had about it all the qualities of an absolute epic. Jackie Stewart and Jochen Rindt were now more closely matched than at any time previously in their careers, going out to do battle at Silverstone armed with the Ford Cosworth-powered Matra MS80 and Lotus 49B respectively.

Just over five years had passed since that memorable day in the spring sunshine at Crystal Palace. They were years in which Rindt should have won races, but didn't. With Cooper from 1965 to the end of 1967, he drove the unreliable Brabham-Repco V8 in 1968 before he finally switched to Lotus.

In the light of the tragedy to come, it is important to realise precisely what sort of a relationship Rindt

would develop with Lotus boss Colin Chapman. Jim Clark had been killed at Hockenheim in the spring of 1968 and Chapman wanted a real charger to lead the team the following year. As a driver, Rindt fitted the bill, but he wasn't emotionally on the same wavelength as the Lotus chief. In 1968, Rindt had trusted Jack Brabham totally, but in 1969 his partnership with Chapman would be much more hard and businesslike.

Chapman had regarded Jim Clark as a close friend. They talked the same language and enjoyed an almost telepathic degree of communication when it came to technical matters. And Jimmy was the ultimate car conserver: smooth, delicate of touch, an overwhelmingly natural driver. After his death, Graham Hill had done his best to sustain Team Lotus's fortunes and won the 1968 World

Championship, but closer scrutiny of his results reveals just how lucky he was to have beaten Jackie Stewart's Matra, now very much the F1 pacemaker.

By the time the summer of 1969 came around, Stewart and Rindt were F1's top dogs. Jochen's arrival at Lotus resulted in the eclipse of Graham Hill's fortunes. He may have been reigning World Champion, but Chapman knew Rindt was his number one hope in the battle against Stewart and the superb French-built Matra. Their rivalry came to a head in the British Grand Prix at Silverstone.

Watched by an estimated 100,000-strong crowd, Rindt and Stewart rocketed off the line like never before. Jochen got through the first couple of corners ahead, leading Jackie's Matra out on to the Hangar Straight with John Surtees third in the revamped BRM P139. As the field braked for Stowe,

this trio became a twosome as Surtees's car broke a front suspension wishbone, forcing its pursuers to take avoiding action, which allowed Rindt and Stewart to pull clear.

On lap six, Stewart found a gap and nipped through into the lead, but eight laps later Rindt went back ahead. Now Jackie had to pull out every stop possible to keep pace.

"In those days, we slipstreamed a lot round places like Silverstone," recalled the Scot 25 years after that epic battle. "Jochen and I had cars which were pretty evenly matched that day and we signalled to each other where to pass and repass. There was no point in blocking each other, because that would have let the others close up, so we ran in the closest possible company, knowing full well that we could totally trust each other."

Jochen Rindt splashes to third place in the 1968 German GP in his Brabham-Repco, the only high spot in an otherwise bleak season.

Just as it looked as though Rindt at last had his first Grand Prix win in the bag, Stewart could see his friend was in trouble. One of the rear wing end plates on the Lotus 49B was working loose, threatening to foul a rear tyre. Obviously worried, Stewart pulled alongside and signalled to Jochen.

"At Silverstone that day, Jochen was the epitome of smoothness and elegance behind the wheel and as good a driver as I have ever raced against," recalls Jackie. "We both drove cars which handled well and it was one of the best races of my life as far as memories are concerned."

"But it was never allowed to reach a conclusion. The end plate of his rear wing came undone and began rubbing against a rear tyre. Jochen and I were very good friends, so I was a little confused as to how to play it. We could obviously communicate to a very limited extent, and I was left with the dilemma of deciding whether to tell him about something which was potentially very dangerous. But would he think that here was Jackie either trying to fool him, or take advantage, or what?"

"In the end I did pull alongside on the Hangar Straight and point at his problem in the hope that he would be able to see it in his rear-view mirror and make his own judgement. Jochen did in fact stop to have the end plate ripped off, resuming about 30 seconds behind me, in a strong second place. He later made a second stop for fuel, which dropped him to fourth."

"That was a hell of a race, but it was with a driver who had undoubtedly matured. There was a man who had extraordinary natural talent, but who was able to recognise that its uninhibited use was an unsuccessful method of driving. What he had to do was harness that enormous natural gift by mental aptitude."

Without that second delay, Rindt might still have been in with a chance at Silverstone, but, as Jackie remembers above, a few laps from the finish the Lotus began misfiring, low on fuel. The furious Austrian had to stop yet again for a top-up but just managed to pip Piers Courage for fourth place behind Ickx and McLaren on the very last lap.

Jochen lived for only 13 months after that epic race at Silverstone. He won his first Grand Prix victory at Watkins Glen later in 1969, then the following year won the Monaco, Dutch, French, British and German Grands Prix, the last four with Chapman's superbly innovative Lotus 72.

On Saturday 5 September 1970, Jochen went out to practice his Lotus 72 in preparation for the Italian Grand Prix at Monza. At Chapman's insistence, he was running without nose wings or rear aerofoil in an attempt to squeeze as much straightline speed as possible out of the car to counter the more powerful flat-12 Ferraris. Rindt's teammate John Miles was told that he had to do the same, but reported that the car felt horrifyingly unstable in such a configuration.

Braking for the Parabolica corner, Rindt lost control when one of the shafts operating the inboard front brakes fractured. He hit the barrier and suffered fatal, multiple injuries. He never lived to know that he was the 1970 World Champion, the sport's only posthumous title holder to this day.

Jackie Stewart was bereft. Only twelve months earlier, he had clinched his own first World Championship here at Monza, beating Jochen's Lotus to the chequered flag by half a car's length after a fantastic wheel-to-wheel battle which again illustrated their absolute mutual trust. Now his close friend was dead and he still had to go out and race the following day.

At the wheel of the uncompetitive Tyrrell team March 701, Stewart threw himself into the contest with total commitment to finish an exhausted second behind Clay Regazzoni's Ferrari. He would race on for three more seasons, winning two more World Championships in 1971 and 1973, and then retire from the cockpit at the age of 34. After Rindt's death, he admitted, motor racing was never quite the same for him again.

> "At Silverstone that day, Jochen was the epitome of smoothness and elegance behind the wheel and as good a driver as I have ever raced," recalls Jackie.

Jochen Rindt's Lotus (No 2) is slow away from the start at Hockenheim during the 1970 German GP. He would eventually pip the Ferrari of Jacky Ickx (No 10) to score the last race victory of his career. Less than two months later he was killed at the wheel of this Lotus at Monza.

4 lauda and hunt

opposites
attract

On the morning of the 1976 Canadian Grand Prix, James Hunt was dozing quietly in his hotel bedroom when the door burst open. The Englishman blinked through tired eyes to take in the sight of his rival and friend Niki Lauda, fully dressed in his racing overalls and crash helmet. Without any preliminaries, Lauda goose-stepped in, announced, "Today I am going to win zee World Championship," and then goose-stepped out again, back into his own adjoining room. In years to come, Hunt would recount that story with glee, for although they were pitched together in one of the closest World Championship battles of the decade, James and Niki remained friends throughout.

Niki Lauda, making his mark at the wheel of the BRM P160 in the 1973 Spanish Grand Prix.

Previous page: Friends and rivals. Hunt and Lauda were great pals out of the car.

James Hunt and Niki Lauda first came together as rivals in the international racing milieu during 1971. James was the Wellington-educated son of a London stockbroker, Niki the scion of a wealthy Viennese family who had banking and transport interests. Both men started out in motor racing with little support from their parents, and both made it to the international front rank thanks to their own determination and application.

Outwardly, they were very different individuals, but they were fired by much the same competitive passion. Hunt was tousle-haired, muscular, with a gregarious, extrovert nature; jeans and tee-shirts made up most of his off-track wardrobe.

By contrast, Lauda was slim and wiry, given to wearing timeless corduroys, loafers and grey crew-neck pullovers. He was also naturally quiet and unemotional, although early exposure to the British motor-racing community revealed he had a dry, ironic wit lurking just below the surface of his character. Yet James and Niki hit it off from the start.

Lauda cut his teeth in European Formula Vee single seaters, then tried Formula 3 before investing £8500 in renting a drive with the fledgling March company in the 1971 European F2 Championship. Hunt started in British F3 in 1969 and finally made it to the works March F3 team a couple of years later. He had a single March F2 outing that year, at Brands Hatch, where he and Niki wound up arguing over who was going to have a freshly rebuilt engine in their car for the race.

Even so, the two youngsters knocked about together in London, where both rented flats a few miles apart. In 1972, Niki successfully raised some

more sponsorship to race in Formula 1 for March, but the cars were hopelessly uncompetitive and it seemed likely the young Austrian would sink without trace. Hunt, meanwhile, stayed in the works F3 team until he was fired in the middle of the season after overdriving and crashing too frequently in a similarly uncompetitive machine.

Lauda also kept his hand in driving F2 for March, with rather more success, and by the end of the year Hunt had clawed his way back into the same category in a year-old March operated by the extrovert Lord Hesketh. So James and Niki squared up to each other in a handful of F2 races before the end of the season. The outcome of these confrontations was inconclusive, but there was more to come in 1973.

Hesketh was keen to continue backing Hunt in Formula 2, but after some troubled outings with a Surtees TS15, his Lordship decided to go the whole hog, buy a March Grand Prix car and contest the World Championship. Meanwhile, Lauda had skilfully manipulated his way into the BRM works team and the two pals arrived on a Grand Prix grid together for the first time in that year's Monaco Grand Prix.

Niki had scored his first championship points with a fifth place in the Belgian Grand Prix, then ran an impressive third in the BRM P160 at Monaco until sidelined by gearbox problems. James got up

One year on, Lauda the winner for Ferrari in the 1974 Spanish race.

to sixth in the Hesketh March until engine failure sidelined him shortly before the finish. Sure, Lauda had more experience, but the BRM was generally uncompetitive and Hunt's March a more agile, reliable technical package.

By mid-season Hunt was gaining momentum. He finished fourth in the British Grand Prix at Silverstone, third in the Dutch at Zandvoort and rounded off the year with a brilliant second to Ronnie Peterson's pace-setting Lotus in the US Grand Prix at Watkins Glen. He finished his first F1 season eighth in the World Championship with 14 points, but Niki's two points in Belgium were all he earned, so he wound up 17th.

Hunt remained with Hesketh for the next two seasons, while Lauda engineered a switch to the famous Ferrari squad. Admittedly, James had the all-new, tailor-made Hesketh 308 to drive from the start of 1974, but it was no match for the superbly reliable Ferrari 312B3 which Niki now had at his disposal. James scored his first Formula 1 victory in

the non-championship Silverstone International Trophy, but Lauda won two Grands Prix in the Ferrari and went into the 1975 season aiming for the World Championship.

Their friendship was standing up remarkably well under the strain of their professional rivalry, and indeed would continue to do so. But during 1975 it was possible to detect a mounting sense of frustration on Hunt's part.

He had matured as a driver over the previous two seasons, benefiting enormously from the calm tutelage of Hesketh team manager 'Bubbles' Horsley. Now he figured he had the right balance between aggressiveness and tactical know-how to win races, but the Ford-powered Hesketh was not quite a match for the opposition. His frustration was heightened by the fact that Lauda was now reeling off the wins on his way to what turned out to be the first of three World Championships.

For Hunt, the great breakthrough eventually came at Zandvoort in the Dutch Grand Prix.

James Hunt in the Hesketh 308 on his way to victory in the 1975 Dutch Grand Prix at Zandvoort.

Left: Hunt showers the bubbly while Lauda makes do with second place after James's Dutch GP win.

Getting serious. Lauda's Ferrari 312T2 leads Hunt's McLaren M23 in the opening stages of the 1976 British GP at Brands Hatch. James got through to win on the road, but was later disqualified and Niki inherited the win.

Starting in heavy rain, the track gradually dried out and Hunt gained an early advantage due to a tactically well-timed tyre change. In the second half of the race, Niki came at him hard, the more powerful Ferrari cutting into the Hesketh's advantage, pressuring James all the way to the chequered flag. But Hunt never put a wheel out of place and stormed home to a great victory. Later, James said he wasn't too worried about Niki's presence in his mirrors; he suspected Lauda would be content with second place, more concerned about gathering championship points than forcing the issue to win the race.

At the end of the season, Niki duly celebrated his first World Championship with five wins to his credit. Added to the two he had amassed in 1974, he now had seven Grand Prix victories under his belt. James just had the one. Worse, he soon began to appreciate there was little chance of Lord Hesketh raising sufficient commercial sponsorship to continue in F1 for 1976.

Hunt's Hesketh fends off Lauda's Ferrari at Zandvoort in 1975.

So it proved. Hesketh withdrew from front-line Formula 1, but James was thrown a lifeline when twice-World Champion Emerson Fittipaldi shocked the Grand Prix world by quitting the McLaren team to drive for the Brazilian Copersucar outfit run by his brother Wilson. Hunt was the logical candidate for the vacant McLaren drive and the deal was quickly done. Now he would be able to take on Lauda, his old friend, in a straight fight with comparable equipment.

The 1976 World Championship season proved to be one of the most remarkable in the sport's history. Lauda opened with two wins and seemed on course to retain his title. But the Ferrari team's initial advantage was not sustained. After wins in Brazil, South Africa, Belgium and Monaco, the Italians suddenly found themselves stalled in the fast lane. Mechanical unreliability intervened at the French Grand Prix and Niki was comprehensively outpaced by James in the British race at Brands Hatch.

This was a controversial race, having been red-flagged to a halt after a multiple pile-up at Paddock Bend on the opening lap. Initially the race stewards would not permit Hunt to take the restart, uncon-

Right: Lauda's Ferrari leads Hunt in the 1976 Spanish Grand Prix. James won here, was disqualified, and later reinstated.

vinced that he was still running when the red flag went out, but thanks to some vociferous, nationalistic support from the grandstands, they reversed their decision.

Niki led from the restart, but James soon slashed his advantage and sliced past, under-braking for Druids hairpin to take over at the head of the pack. This manoeuvre was fascinating in itself: Lauda left just enough room, and no more, for Hunt to squeeze the McLaren inside his Ferrari. It was a classic example of the give-and-take which characterized the way top drivers operated in those days. The thought of deliberately provoking a collision was simply out of the question.

At the end of the race, Niki was still leading the World Championship by 58 points to James's 35. His Ferrari then crashed in flames early in the German Grand Prix at Nurburgring. The race was stopped, Lauda was rescued from the conflagration and helicoptered off to hospital in Cologne, apparently close to death.

Niki quits the 1976 Japanese Grand Prix; a brave decision under the circumstances.

Hunt, obviously concerned about his friend, took the restart and won commandingly in his McLaren. Niki then made a quite remarkable recovery to return to the cockpit, his blistered scalp swathed in bandages, for the Italian GP at Monza barely eight weeks later. Niki still led from Hunt, but with only 61 points to the Englishman's 56.

Then came the body blow. The governing body's court of appeal disqualified James from his British Grand Prix victory. The revised points position was now Niki on 64, James on 47. And there were three races to go.

What followed were probably Hunt's two best-ever Grand Prix wins. With the pressure increasingly stacked against him, he had no choice but to go for broke in the Canadian and United States races. He won them both, displaying exactly the right blend of skill and aggressive forcefulness to eclipse all his rivals.

In the aftermath of the appeal court ruling, relations between Niki and James became a little tense

and waspish. But it was nothing serious or long-term, merely a reflection of the acutely stressed circumstances in which they found themselves.

The championship clincher would now be the Japanese Grand Prix at the Mount Fuji circuit, an event which took place in torrential rain. Lauda qualified third, just behind Hunt, but had used up all his resilience in battling his injuries. The prospect of racing on a flooded track just did not seem worth it and he withdrew from the race after only a couple of laps. He made no excuses, he just wasn't prepared to race in those conditions.

Hunt survived a late race puncture, and consequent hurried tyre change, to bring his McLaren

This manoeuvre was fascinating in itself: Lauda left just enough room, and no more, for Hunt to squeeze the McLaren inside his Ferrari. It was a classic example of the give-and-take which characterized the way drivers operated in those days.

home third behind Mario Andretti's Lotus and Patrick Depailler's Tyrrell. He was World Champion by the margin of a single point, but was quick to acknowledge his rival's achievement. "I think Niki Lauda is the bravest man I have ever known," he said firmly in the immediate aftermath of the race.

Twelve months after that decisive race, James Hunt returned to the Mount Fuji circuit to win the 1977 Japanese Grand Prix. He was not to know that this would be the final victory of his career. By then Niki Lauda had silenced his many critics and bounced back to win a second championship, retaking the title from James.

For 1978, Niki switched to the Brabham-Alfa Romeo team. A year later, James withdrew from the McLaren ranks and signed for the team owned by Austro-Canadian oil magnate Walter Wolf. After the Monaco Grand Prix, James decided to retire from motor racing. Later that same season, Niki followed suit – quitting mid-way through practice for the Canadian Grand Prix at Montreal. Both felt they were played out, no longer sufficiently motivated to compete at the top level.

Hunt settled into a relaxed, slightly Bohemian lifestyle in the leafy enclave of Wimbledon, south London, not really knowing what he wanted to do

for the rest of his life, but apparently enjoying the wait while he made up his mind. Lauda, the more focused and singleminded of the two, concentrated on expanding his fledgling airline, LaudaAir, and then returned to the F1 cockpit to race on with McLaren from 1982 through to the end of 1985, winning a third championship in 1984. He was older now, more professional than ever and a millionaire with extensive business responsibilities. But Niki still had an enormous amount of time for James, who remained on the Grand Prix scene in his new role as the other half of Murray Walker's double act, commentating on the races for BBC Television.

At the end of a busy day in the cockpit, Lauda would often change out of his overalls and sit outside the team's motorhome, dragging surreptitiously on one of his dreadful cigarillos, to be joined by the chain-smoking Hunt, as often as not barefoot and wearing little more than shorts and singlet.

As they sat there shooting the breeze, the years would fall away and they would giggle conspiratorially, just as they had done over a decade before as F2 hopefuls tilting at the big time. When Lauda heard of Hunt's death, he was simply stunned. " Shit," he said. "James was one of the really great guys." As always, Niki was right on the button.

Lauda's Ferrari leads Jody Scheckter's Wolf and Hunt's McLaren early in the 1977 British GP at Silverstone.

5 villeneuve and pironi

tragic
ending

Of all the partnerships and rivalries recounted in this volume, this was singularly the most unpleasant. More specifically, there are those who believe that the state of personal relations between Ferrari team-mates Gilles Villeneuve and Didier Pironi directly led to the former's tragic death during practice for the 1982 Belgian Grand Prix at Zolder.

The story started in 1981 when Pironi, then 27 years old, joined Ferrari as Villeneuve's team-mate. A dour, calculating Frenchman who projected a flatly unemotional personality, Pironi was totally consumed by the desire to become his country's first ever World Champion driver. To that end, he applied a clinical and objective strategy to the business of his motor racing, seemingly always keeping his temperament and emotions under tight rein in public.

The young Pironi had benefited enormously from the French motor-racing infra-structure of the 1970s which, largely thanks to the financial clout of the Elf petroleum group, carefully prepared its most promising young stars for Formula 1 stardom by chanelling them through the junior single-seater formulae.

By 1977, Pironi stood on the threshold of the Grand Prix business, having won the Monaco Formula 3 classic that year on a guest outing for the Martini team. This attracted the attention of British team boss Ken Tyrrell – whose team was at that time sponsored by Elf – and Didier Pironi duly joined fellow Frenchman Patrick Depailler in their line-up for 1978.

Pironi proved his talent by scoring championship points in four out of his first six races for Tyrrell – and also won the Le Mans 24-hour sports car classic, driving for Renault. In fact, France's national racing team wanted to sign him up for 1979, but Tyrrell was not interested in selling his contract. So he spent another, largely fruitless, year driving for Tyrrell before switching to the Ligier squad in 1980.

> There were two weeks now until the Championship battle resumed at Zolder for the Belgian Grand Prix. During that time, Villeneuve was eaten up with dismay and disbelief over Pironi's behaviour. This gentle, principled man firmly believed he had been fundamentally betrayed by his team-mate.

As Pironi made steady progress through the ranks, Gilles Villeneuve was busy consolidating his image as one of the most exciting drivers ever to be put behind the wheel of a Ferrari. The French-Canadian had come to international prominence back in 1976 when he won the Canadian national Formula Atlantic race on the demanding Trois Rivieres street circuit on the banks of the St Lawrence river. James Hunt was also having a guest outing in that race and, having been comprehensively trounced by Villeneuve, came straight back to England and told the McLaren team to keep a firm eye on this young charger.

Villeneuve was duly given his Formula 1 break in the 1977 British Grand Prix at the wheel of a third works McLaren. Yet thanks to an alarming lack of perspicacity on the part of the team's management, when it came to replacing Hunt's team-mate Jochen Mass at the end of the season, they opted for Frenchman Patrick Tambay instead. However, McLaren's loss was Ferrari's gain and in 1978 Gilles went to the famous Italian team, where he proved an instant hit and scored his first Grand Prix win in the 1978 Canadian race before his delighted home crowd at Montreal.

In 1979, Gilles finished runner-up to his team-mate Jody Scheckter in the Drivers' World Championship. To that end, he drove the entire Italian Grand Prix in second place behind Scheckter, knowing that all he had to do to win the title was overtake the South African. But Gilles was abiding scrupulously, religiously, by team orders. In his mind, had he won the championship underhandedly, it would have been a valueless achievement.

In 1980, Ferrari had a dismal season and failed to win a single race, whereas Pironi successfully broke his Formula 1 duck by winning the Belgian Grand Prix at Zolder in the Ligier. However, this was the start of F1's turbo era and Ferrari had a formidably

Previous page: Villeneuve and Pironi amongst their colleagues at the pre-race driver briefing, Imola, 1982.

Playing it by the book. Villeneuve shadows Jody Scheckter in a Ferrari 1-2 at Monza in the 1979 Italian Grand Prix, which saw the South African driver clinch the championship.

promising new turbocharged engine in the pipeline for 1981. It looked a good bet, so when Scheckter retired from racing at the end of the 1980 season, Pironi did not take much in the way of tempting to sign up as Villeneuve's team-mate for 1981.

Villeneuve scored two brilliant victories that season, in the Monaco and Spanish Grands Prix. On both occasions, Pironi was nowhere. In fact, at Monaco, Gilles left him trailing in a lapped fourth place at the chequered flag. Whether this began to sow the seeds of resentment in the Frenchman's mind is difficult to say. The two men always seemed to get on well enough, despite their contrasting temperaments. Villeneuve was cautiously gregarious, up-front. What you saw was what you got. Somehow Pironi was more reticent, like a gambler who was unwilling to show his hand.

The disastrous confrontation between the two men would come at the 1982 San Marino Grand Prix at Imola, a race which Ferrari effectively had to itself after the event was boycotted by the British-based teams aligned with the influential Formula One Constructors' Association. FOCA was in dispute with the sport's governing body, the FISA, over the interpretation and enforcement of certain technical regulations. For the moment, they had reached an impasse and stayed away.

In the end, a far from full field of 14 cars turned out to contest the race. Pole position fell to Rene Arnoux's Renault turbo ahead of Alain Prost's sister car, with Villeneuve and Pironi side-by-side on the second row in their Ferrari 126C2 turbos. Throughout practice, both Ferrari drivers had complained to their engineers about poor grip and excessive wheelspin, but remained pretty confident about their prospects for the race. Either way, as far as the paying public was concerned, a small field was a matter of no concern as long as the scarlet Italian cars were on the grid. This was the Autodromo Enzo e Dino Ferrari, after all.

Come the start, things didn't look too promising for the Maranello team. Arnoux went straight into the lead and began to pull away, his Renault demonstrating obviously superior traction and

Pironi was in a class of his own on this occasion with the Ligier which usually found itself beaten by the more reliable Williams FW07B.

Left: Didier Pironi leads the pack at Zolder in the 1980 Belgian Grand Prix, which he won commandingly for the Ligier team. The following year he joined Villeneuve at Ferrari.

straight-line speed. However, Prost dropped away with a sick engine almost from the opening lap, so it was clear there was still something of a question mark hanging over Renault's technical reliability. In any event, with 20 laps completed, the two Ferraris had closed up on Arnoux and the fans were being treated to a gripping three-way battle for the lead.

The two Ferraris were clearly racing each other with as much ferocity as the Renault. On lap 26, the crowd went wild with delight as Villeneuve took the

lead for the first time. He stayed ahead for four laps, then Arnoux went back in front. Then Pironi slipped through into second place as the Renault began trailing smoke. On lap 45 – with 15 left to run – Arnoux pulled off with a failed turbocharger. Villeneuve now led from Pironi.

However, this was not the end of Ferrari's problems. The fuel-hungry turbocharged engines were slurping the contents of their tanks at a prodigious rate. Running first and second on home soil, the

Tragic sequel. Didier Pironi at Hockenheim, 1982, just before the accident which would end his motor-racing career for good.

team simply could not afford the ignominy of their cars running out of fuel. Consequently the team manager hung out a 'SLOW' sign to both men, directing them to ease back on the throttle and to hold position.

Villeneuve obviously thought of Monza in 1979. He knew that standing orders meant that Ferrari team drivers must keep position at the point they took over first and second place in any race. Logically, he figured that this would be his victory.

Although the two cars continued to swap places all round the circuit, Villeneuve was happy to play the game. He was confident that, on this occasion, victory was in the bag.

Going into the final lap, Villeneuve was back in the lead. "I was running so easily, you just can't believe it," he said later. "I was cruising along and believed that Pironi was being honest. I was not expecting him to pass me again, but all of a sudden I saw him coming up on me. He slid past with all wheels locked, and that was the end of it."

Pironi had carried off a hair-raising maneouvre in his determination to take the lead. He pulled out of Villeneuve's slipstream at around 185mph as they slammed through the fast right-hand kink into the braking area for the Tosa hairpin. His Ferrari weaved dramatically as the Frenchman almost lost control, but he gathered it up successfully to emerge in the lead as they accelerated out of the bend.

All hope of a Villeneuve counter-attack was now gone. Only half a lap remained and the two Ferraris crossed the line 0.4 seconds apart with Pironi ahead. The body language on the winner's rostrum told the whole story. Villeneuve could not bring himself to look at Pironi, much less congratulate him. When the official proceedings were over, Gilles absented himself as quickly as possible.

Pironi made a half-hearted attempt to pour oil on

Gilles Villeneuve on the last day of his life, practising the Ferrari 126C2 at Zolder in preparation for the 1982 Belgian Grand Prix.

troubled waters. "We both had engine problems and, no, there were no team orders,"he claimed lamely. But Villeneuve would have none of that. In front of the media, he told it as it was. "What he says is just not true. Ever since I've been at Ferrari, when you get a 'slow' sign it means 'hold position.' Second is one thing, but second because he steals it, that's something else."

There were two weeks now until the championship battle resumed at Zolder for the Belgian Grand Prix. During that time, Villeneuve was eaten up with dismay and disbelief over Pironi's behaviour. This gentle, principled man firmly believed he had been fundamentally betrayed by his team-mate. From now on, he vowed, he would regard Pironi's as just another racing car to be beaten.

An insight into Villeneuve's mood during the days after the Imola race was gained by *Autosport* columnist Nigel Roebuck. Villeneuve told him:

"After the race I thought that everyone would realise what had happened, but not. Pironi says that we both had engine problems and that there were no team orders, and what really pissed me off was that Piccinini [the Ferrari team manager] confirmed that to the press.

"My engine was perfect. People seemed to think we'd had the battle of our lives! Jesus Christ! I'd been ahead of him for most of the race, qualified a second and a half quicker than him. Where was my problem? I was coasting those last 15 laps; he was racing. I think I've proved that, in equal cars, if I want someone to stay behind me...well, I think he stays behind."

Asked if he would stay with Ferrari into 1983, Villeneuve replied that he was uncertain. However, if Pironi was to stay there, then no way. Clearly, Villeneuve's attitude was sufficiently trenchant to provoke a reaction from Enzo Ferrari himself. On

the Tuesday after the Imola race, he took an unprecedented step by issuing a press release on the matter. The bottom line was that he came down solidly in Villeneuve's favour.

Two weeks later, while practising for the Grand Prix at Zolder, Villeneuve went out in an effort to beat Pironi's slightly faster time in qualifying. Midway round his next flying lap, a dawdling March driven by Jochen Mass strayed into his path. Unwilling to lift from the throttle, Villeneuve ducked right, just as Mass moved right across the nose of his Ferrari.

Villeneuve's car was launched over Mass's left rear wheel and came crashing down into a gravel trap on the right-hand side of the circuit before cart-

Asked if he would stay with Ferrari into the 1983 season, Villeneuve replied that he was uncertain. However, if Pironi was to stay there, then no way.

wheeling to destruction on the other side of the circuit. Gilles was flung out and sustained injuries from which he died a few hour later. Since Imola, he had not exchanged so much as a single word with Didier Pironi.

Ironically, the Frenchman's racing career lasted only a few months more. While practising for the German Grand Prix at Hockenheim, Pironi was running in heavy rain and spray when his Ferrari too was vaulted over the back of Alain Prost's McLaren, which had proved virtually invisible in the appalling conditions. His legs shattered, Pironi had to undergo many painful operations before he could even walk again.

A return to the cockpit of a racing car was now out of the question, so he took to the equally spectacular sport of powerboat racing in an adrenalin substitute. In August 1987 he hurtled through the wake of a passing tanker off the Isle of Wight without easing back the throttles. The powerboat flipped over, killing Pironi and his two crew members. A few weeks later, his girlfriend would give birth to twin sons, one of whom she named Gilles.

Gilles Villeneuve on the last day of his life, practising the Ferrari 126C2 at Zolder in preparation for the 1982 Belgian GP.

6 prost and lauda

new stars
for old

By the end of 1981, Niki Lauda realised that he missed Grand Prix racing dreadfully. His retirement from the sport midway through a practice session for the 1979 Canadian Grand Prix had left him with plenty to do in terms of business, but the challenge of expanding his airline, LaudaAir, left him only partly fulfilled. Moreover, throughout his retirement, McLaren team chief Ron Dennis had been discreetly probing him on the question of a possible return to the cockpit.

auda was eventually tempted to test a McLaren at the end of the 1981 season and concluded that a return was feasible. So he did a deal with McLaren, on the strict understanding that they could dispense with his services four races into the 1982 season if he did not turn out to be sufficiently competitive. As things transpired, Niki won the third race of his return, the US Grand Prix West through the streets of Long Beach, California, to emphasise that he had certainly not lost his touch.

Through 1982 and 1983, Niki successfully kept the upper hand at McLaren over team-mate John Watson, the man who had won the revived team's first Grand Prix at Silverstone back in 1981. Meanwhile, Dennis had lavish plans to establish McLaren as an undisputed World Championship contender. With financial support from the Franco-Saudi high-technology company TAG, McLaren commissioned Porsche to design and build a state-of-the-art turbocharged Formula 1 engine which would be ready for use in the closing stages of the 1983 season.

In fact, Lauda used the new engine in the final race of that season, the South African Grand Prix at Kyalami, and was closing in on eventual race winner Riccardo Patrese's Brabham when forced to retire with fuel system problems. Yet he had seen enough to convince himself that he might well be in a position to challenge for his third World Championship the following year, particularly with Watson still on hand to drive the second car.

Unfortunately, Niki's carefully nurtured calculations went straight out of the window almost within days of the last race of 1983. Watson over-played

his hand in negotiations with McLaren over the terms of his contract for the following year, so Ron Dennis moved quickly when Alain Prost suddenly came on to the driver market.

Prost was effectively being made the fall-guy for Renault's failure to win the 1983 World Championship, despite the fact that it was clear to all concerned that the French company had not realised its ambition due to an inability to respond to BMW's engine development programme for the rival Brabham team, which eventually pipped them to the title.

Lauda found himself inwardly cursing his luck. He'd already seen enough of Prost to realise that his new team-mate was likely to offer formidable competition. With that in mind, he drew on all his resources, personal and contractual, to gain a performance edge. To start with, Niki exercised what he considered his *droit du seigneur* when it came to pre-season testing with the new car. On several occasions Alain would find himself kicking his heels in the pits while Niki did as much development work as he chose, sometimes not relinquishing the test car until late on a particular afternoon so that

Alain and Niki: one of the greatest F1 partnerships of all time.

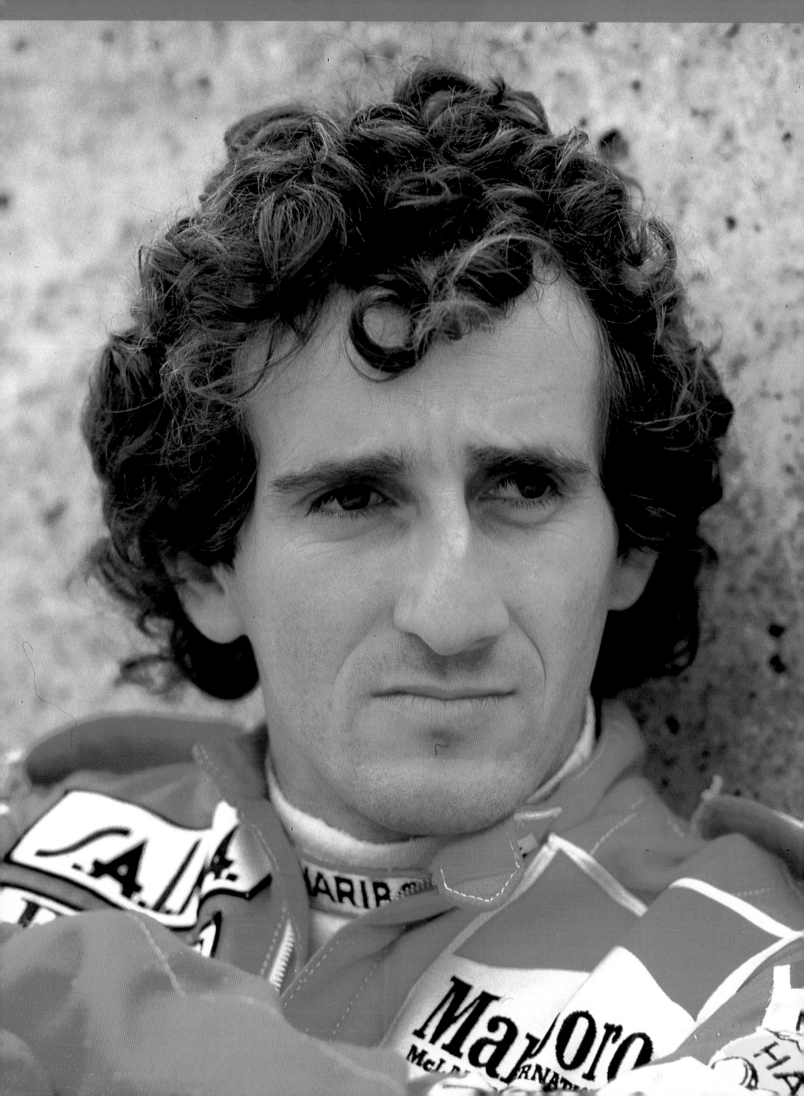

Alain Prost's McLaren accelerates away from the start of the 1984 British GP at Brands Hatch ahead of Nelson Piquet's Brabham, Niki Lauda's McLaren and Derek Warwick's Renault.

Alain's time behind the wheel would be restricted.

Off track, there were other potential problems. Although it took some time before Niki convinced himself that Prost's apparent hero worship of him was genuine, he was aware of mounting tension with Ron Dennis. After their maiden season together in 1982, Niki had negotiated a highly lucrative two-year deal for 1983 and 1984 worth many millions of dollars. Given Prost's situation, however, the Frenchman had no options when he signed for McLaren in 1984. By comparison with Niki, he was paid peanuts. And as he gradually asserted himself as the more convincing performer, so Dennis became slightly irked at the inequality surrounding this anomaly.

One thing, however, was beyond dispute. The new TAG turbo engine was highly competitive and the 1984 McLarens quickly became the class of the field. More to the point, Prost staked his claim to de facto team leadership by winning the first race of the season in Brazil. Niki bounced back by winning in South Africa, round two of the title chase, but Prost had to take the spare car and start from the pit lane after his race car suffered mechanical problems just before the off. But it was not really a representative performance by the Austrian.

At the end of the day, Niki relied on guile, racecraft and the experience built up throughout more than a decade of Grand Prix racing. He freely admitted that he was getting a little too old to take the sort of risks Prost was prepared to go for in traffic; dodging through gaps which didn't seem to be there to the older, more seasoned campaigner. As often as not, Niki would concentrate much of his

Left: Alain Prost; McLaren's new star in the making.

efforts in practice on sorting out the car in preparation for the race. This was his forte and he reaped the benefit.

Lauda won again in France, Britain, Austria and Italy. Prost was first past the flag in the Netherlands, Germany, San Marino, Canada and Monaco, the last-mentioned race being flagged to a stop in heavy rain at half distance. Half points were awarded and Prost collected only four and a half points rather than the usual nine. Had this race gone its full distance, Alain's first championship would have been in the bag.

In all these stories of great rivalry and competition, there is a key event, a single race, which seems to capture the fundamental essence of the relationship. If for Pironi and Villeneuve it was the 1982 San Marino GP, so – in a much happier way – for Lauda and Prost the moment of truth was the final round of the 1984 World Championship, the Portuguese Grand Prix at Estoril.

A title secured, Lauda commiserates with Prost on the victory rostrum at Estoril in 1984.

Both men went into the race capable of winning the title. You could have reached out and cut the tension. Lauda went into the Estoril race with 66 points, Prost with 62.5. Thus if Alain won, he would end up with a total of 71.5 points. If that happened, then Niki would have to finish second – thereby gaining a season total of 72 points – to prevent his team-mate taking the title. It all seemed hypothetical in the extreme, particularly as the Austrian could only manage 11th place on the grid after a troubled

qualifying session. Alain was second, alongside Nelson Piquet's pole position Brabham-BMW.

At the start, Keke Rosberg's Williams-Honda catapulted into an immediate lead to head the pack at the end of the opening lap from Nigel Mansell's Lotus-Renault and a circumspect Prost. Niki was down in 11th, apparently boxed in by the unruly, jostling, midfield pack.

On the second lap, Prost moved ahead of Mansell to take second place. Seven laps later, he neatly outbraked Rosberg for the lead and began to ease away from the pack. At this point, it hardly looked as though Lauda had a hope in hell.

As Alain paced himself steadily at the front of the field, so Niki gradually ducked and dived his way through the traffic. But even as he did so, his experience told him that something was not quite right with his engine performance. The F1 cars of the time had controls in the cockpit whereby the amount of turbo boost to the engine could be stepped up momentarily to provide a little more power for overtaking. But this was costly in terms of fuel consumption and shrewd racers like Lauda could often turn the boost down to conserve their fuel, taking any extra performance they needed out of the chassis instead.

This time, however, Niki could not feel any difference when he fiddled with the cockpit control. It

Lauda outlasted his team-mate to win the 1984 British GP.

Right: Niki Lauda, the old star, not finished yet.

was frustrating in the extreme, particularly when it came to challenging Swede Stefan Johansson's Toleman for sixth place. The McLaren simply did not respond.

Eventually Lauda took a deep breath and just managed to squeeze by, but it was so tight that the Toleman's nose wing clipped one of the McLaren's rear tyres as Niki pulled back into line. He was lucky to get away without picking up a puncture. Relentlessly, he pulled through the field. On lap 28 he passed Michele Alboreto's Ferrari to take fifth place and then Rosberg succumbed two laps later. On lap 33, he moved in front of Ayrton Senna's third place Toleman and now there was only Nigel Mansell's Lotus separating him from Prost.

Mansell had been driving well, but suddenly found his Lotus abruptly pitched into a spin. He quickly got going again, but something was clearly wrong with the front brakes and he had to pull off

Prost winning the 1984 Dutch GP, one of seven victories that season.

and retire. With 18 laps to run, Lauda now had that third World Championship title in his sights. All he had to do was keep going.

At the end of 70 laps, the chequered flag came out as the two McLarens surged across the line in first and second places, the team's 12th victory of the 16-race season.

As the two drivers mounted the winner's rostrum, Prost was doing his best to stifle tears of disappointment. "Forget it as quickly as you can," Lauda advised him. "Next year the championship will be yours." Prost responded by stepping down from the top position on the podium and beckoning the new World Champion to take his place.

In 1985, Prost and Lauda remained with McLaren, but Niki's car seemed continuously beset by mechanical problems. He still managed to win another race, a close-fought Dutch Grand Prix at Zandvoort in which he unexpectedly cast aside his

precise driving style to throw himself into a frantic battle with Prost, the Austrian emerging a couple of lengths ahead at the chequered flag. In retrospect, it looked like a little bit of fun from a driver who knew he was calling it a day at the end of the season.

Niki Lauda retired for good after the 1985 Australian Grand Prix at Adelaide, a race in which he spun off the road and into a retaining wall when the brakes of his McLaren locked unexpectedly. Niki Lauda had started the trend for front-line Formula 1 comebacks, but this time he was serious about calling it a day.

As Lauda had predicted, Prost won the World Championship in 1985. He went on to win his second title in 1986, then a third in 1989 and, after switching to Williams, a fourth in 1993.

> In retrospect, what made the Prost/Lauda partnership so remarkable was that both men were very similar in their approach to the business of motor racing. Both were intelligent enough to understand that they would make more progress as a team if they worked together in developing the cars.

In retrospect, what made the Prost/Lauda partnership so remarkable was that both men were very similar in their approach to the business of motor racing. And both were intelligent enough to understand that they would make more progress as a team if they worked together in developing the cars.

Prost was a man who appreciated a direct, up-front relationship, and Lauda had about him a streak of outspoken candour which was capable of taking one's breath away. Yet for two memorable Grand Prix seasons they were bound together by a profound sense of mutual professional respect in a highly competitive working environment.

Perhaps even more so than Fangio and Moss, Alain Prost and Niki Lauda made sure things worked out because that was the best way for both of them.

Farewell champ! Lauda, proudly carrying No 1 on his McLaren's nose, surrounded by the pack in his last race, the 1985 Australian GP.

7 mansell and piquet

poles
apart

Nelson Piquet thought that Mansell would be a pushover, an also-ran who had been promoted beyond his ability level. Nigel, meanwhile, regarded the Brazilian as a tactical soft touch who would soon capitulate when faced with pressure from within his own team. It was a recipe for two years of fierce competition between the Williams-Honda team-mates, beginning with the 1985 Austrian Grand Prix. For some weeks, British team chief Frank Williams had been a worried man. His team leader Keke Rosberg was to join rivals McLaren at the end of the season, leaving only Mansell as a confirmed member of the 1986 Williams driver line-up.

Mansell leads the start in Adelaide in 1986 from Senna's Lotus, Piquet and the McLarens of Prost and Rosberg.

Previous page: Before the storm; Mansell with Piquet in 1985, when Nelson was still driving for Brabham.

Williams believes he needs an established number one driver to pair with Mansell. The Englishman has had a promising first season with the team, but Frank has yet to be convinced he is anything more than a competent journeyman, a good number two. So he clinches the deal with Piquet for a figure in the region of $3 million. It is an offer the Brazilian cannot refuse, even though this means turning his back on all his friends in the Brabham team for which he has driven since 1979.

One of the great fascinations of Grand Prix racing is its element of unpredictability. In the few months remaining between Williams signing the deal with Piquet and the end of the 1985 season, Mansell suddenly rang the Formula 1 bell in no uncertain terms. His first victory in the Grand Prix of Europe at Brands Hatch was followed up by another in the South African Grand Prix at Kyalami a few weeks later. By the end of the year, he was being thought of as a possible title challenger.

Piquet was not flustered. Privately, he told friends he didn't feel Mansell was any sort of serious challenge. The powerful new Williams-Honda FW11 looked likely to be the class of the 1986 field and the Brazilian looked forward to winning his third World Championship. Yet events and circumstances would conspire to undermine the certainty of this prediction.

To start with, the team was thrown into some disarray when Frank Williams was badly injured in a road accident just before the start of the season. He was hurrying back to Nice airport to catch a plane back to London at the end of the FW11's final pre-season test and ended up with a broken back, confined to a wheelchair for the rest of his life. He would be out of action for much of the 1986 season whilst making a limited medical recovery and going through the process of adapting himself to these unexpected new circumstances.

Piquet and Mansell thus started the season without Frank to hand – and with Honda, the team's engine supply partner, deeply worried about the apparent loss, however temporary, of an identifiable man in charge at the top of the Williams Grand Prix Engineering management structure.

Nevertheless, the first race of the 1986 season went pretty well to Piquet's predicted plan. Mansell was eliminated in a second-lap collision with Ayrton Senna's Lotus 98T, allowing Piquet an easy stroll through to victory. It was going to be a piece of cake.

Yet suddenly Mansell was on the pace. He came second to Senna's Lotus in the Spanish Grand Prix at Jerez, then won in Belgium, Canada and France to go into his home Grand Prix at Brands Hatch challenging for the championship points lead.

Piquet was by now extremely unhappy at the way events were unfolding; he had, rightly or wrongly, believed that the terms of his contract as Williams's number one driver meant that he would be given preference over Mansell. And by that he felt this didn't just mean priority access to the spare car. It meant keeping Mansell under control and not allowing the two Williams-Hondas to race against each other.

This most certainly was not the way Williams saw it. Piquet's number one status should, in their view, be underpinned by his speed and superior performance over Mansell. They were giving him the

Pressing home the advantage, Mansell leads Piquet in the 1986 British GP at Brands Hatch.

Poised for battle: the Williams team at the start of the 1986 European season.

Right: Nigel Mansell, newly signed by Williams, in 1985.

tools to get the job done and that, they felt, should have been enough.

Matters almost came to a head at the 1986 British Grand Prix where Mansell, the race having been stopped after one lap following a multiple collision at Paddock Bend, took over Piquet's spare car for the restart to beat the Brazilian in a straight fight. Piquet had been leading, but when he fumbled a gearchange, Mansell dodged through to take an emotional home victory. But the tensions were definitely building.

Honda viewed the situation with deep concern. It had poured a considerable investment into the Williams team with a view to powering one of the men behind the wheel to the drivers' title. Yet as Mansell and Piquet continued to race, and take points away from each other, it did not take a mathematical genius to conclude that they could win all the battles, but end up losing the war.

McLaren's Alain Prost was slowly creeping up on both Williams drivers in the title points stake, but when the elderly Soichiro Honda elected to make the trip from Japan to Adelaide for the final race of the season, the Honda founder could still reasonably assume that one of the Williams drivers would take the title.

Mansell qualified superbly on pole position ahead of Piquet, but Ayrton Senna was determined to round off the season with a win for Lotus, even though he knew he was out of the championship equation. Although Mansell led through the first chicane, Senna was hustling him aggressively, knowing full well that Nigel could afford to take no risks in such a strategically delicate situation. In fact, he drove the opening lap of the Australian Grand Prix in such circumspect fashion that he came round fourth behind Senna, Piquet and Keke Rosberg's McLaren.

The crucial slip. Mansell stalls on the grid at Mexico in 1986 and is passed on all sides by the rest of the pack.

This was Rosberg's final F1 race before retirement and he simply disappeared into the middle distance. Senna quickly faded from the equation and by lap 12 the order was Rosberg, Piquet, Alain Prost's McLaren and Mansell. Piquet then spun and dropped behind Mansell, so the title permutations were swerving about in dramatically unpredictable style. It would take until lap 32 for the most crucial development to occur.

Lapping Gerhard Berger's Benetton-BMW, one of Prost's front tyres was punctured when he lightly bumped the Austrian's car. He stopped to have it changed and resumed fourth. Goodyear's technicians had, on the basis of tyre wear during qualifying, been assuming it would be necessary for most of the front runners to make at least one routine

stop during the course of the race. But a quick examination of the tyre which came off Prost's McLaren revealed a much lower wear rate than expected. Word was passed down the pit lane that a non-stop run seemed perfectly feasible.

Then on lap 63, with only 19 left to run, Rosberg's McLaren pulled off at the side of the circuit after a rear tyre failure, a dramatically unexpected occurrence, which caused enormous concern in the pit lane. Piquet and Mansell were now running first and second, but their tyres did not appear to be in good shape in the judgement of the engineers on the pit wall. But before any decision could be made as to whether or not to bring them in for a precautionary stop, the championship favourite's race ended on the very brink of tragedy.

Building up to around 200mph in the slipstream of Philippe Alliot's Ligier as he prepared to lap the Frenchman on Adelaide's long back straight, Mansell's Williams suffered a major failure of its left rear tyre. As the car sat down on that rear corner, Mansell was left battling the wildly zig-zagging machine, wrestling to keep it away from the ominous concrete barriers lining the circuit. He finally came to rest in a slip road, out of the race, his title chances in tatters.

Now Piquet was set for victory, and the championship. But Williams could not take the risk. They called him in for fresh tyres. Ironically, there was no problem; the existing ones were wearing perfectly well. Mansell's failure had been due to an isolated, one-off manufacturing flaw. So Prost was now through into the lead and, despite acute fuel consumption worries, stayed ahead to the chequered flag and retained his championship crown. The Honda management was simply not amused.

The rivalry between Piquet and Mansell had certainly not been improved by the strategic debacle of 1986. The Brazilian found it hard to conceal his contempt and disregard for Mansell; the fact that he had now been proved wrong in his assessment of the Englishman's driving talents simply aggravated those feelings. Mansell, on the other hand, grew to dislike Piquet not only because he was de facto team leader, but also because of the way in which Nelson displayed his obvious ambivalence towards him. They were as oil and water.

Nevertheless, Mansell and Piquet continued to race together as Williams-Honda team-mates through the 1987 World Championship season. But

At the outset, Piquet managed to put his money where his mouth was at Silverstone, edging Mansell out of pole position by less than one-tenth of a second.

Piquet wins at Monza in 1987.

behind the scenes, Honda was making plans to ditch Williams, even though their contract to supply engines officially ran to the end of 1988. Honda had lost faith in the Williams management. They felt that the failure of either Mansell or Piquet to win the 1986 drivers' championship simply underlined this concern.

In parallel with this simmering unease, the personal tension between Mansell and Piquet was also approaching its peak. By the time the two men arrived at Silverstone to begin official qualifying for that year's British Grand Prix, there was precious little common ground left for communications. Only a week before, Mansell had beaten Piquet in a straight fight to win the French Grand Prix at Paul Ricard, after which Nelson went on the record as saying the Englishman had pulled an overtly dangerous maneouvre to take the the lead.

Piquet followed this up by taking a well-aimed swipe at Mansell on his home ground. At a London press conference a few days prior to the Silverstone race, he remarked: "I suppose you could say that while I've won two World Championships, Nigel has only managed to lose one." In Nelson's opinion, going fast and having the tactical acuity to assemble a season-long World Championship winning challenge were not necessarily the same thing.

At the outset, Piquet managed to put his money where his mouth was at Silverstone, edging Mansell out of pole position by less than one-tenth of a second. Both Williams drivers were over a second quicker than the opposition, so it was set to be a repeat of Brands Hatch the previous year. Nothing but a two-horse race.

Accelerating away from the start, the two Williams drivers were so absorbed in trying to intimidate each other by attempting to rub wheels that they completely took their eye off the ball and left sufficient space for Prost's McLaren-TAG to come sprinting down the outside and take an immediate lead. This lasted only a couple of corners, however, before Piquet and Mansell surged past into first and second places.

As Piquet began to edge clear at the head of the pack, so the question of tyre stops began to loom on the horizon. Before the start, Williams had finalized a strategy whereby they would signal to both their drivers when they had reached the 35-lap point in the 65-lap race. Then it would be up to both Nigel and Nelson to make a decision as to whether or not they wanted to stop for fresh rubber.

Ominously, after about 15 laps, Mansell began to be bothered by a front wheel vibration. It later transpired this had been triggered by a lost wheel balance weight, but it certainly prompted Mansell to decide that he would come in for new tyres at the end of lap 35. He duly did so, accelerating back into the fray after his car was at rest for only 9.2 seconds.

As at Adelaide the previous autumn, the intervention of the Goodyear tyre technicians played a central role in the outcome of the race. They examined the tyres which had come off Mansell's car and then gave Williams the thumbs-up. 'TYRES OK' was the sign held over the pit wall to Piquet, who pressed on, confident and reassured.

Left: Still smiling. Piquet in his first season with Williams, 1986.

Mansell practising at Suzuka for the 1987 Japanese GP before the crash which caused him to withdraw from the race, thus handing the World Championship to Piquet.

Best of enemies, 1987.

However, Mansell was now benefiting from the added grip afforded by his new tyres. With 25 laps to go he started slicing into Piquet's lead. On lap 48, Nelson was 16.8 seconds ahead, but by lap 56 it was down to 6.3 seconds, then 3.9, then 2.8.

Piquet knew only too well that he could expect no assistance from the Williams pits and, on lap 63, Mansell tricked him into moving the wrong way as they slammed down the Hangar Straight at 190mph into the braking area for the tricky Stowe Corner. Throwing caution to the wind, Mansell kept his foot hard on the throttle all the way to his second straight British Grand Prix win, taking the chequered flag 1.9 seconds ahead of his team-mate. Then he ran out of fuel on the slowing-down lap!

Despite all the Mansell mania of another home win, few observers could have failed to notice Nelson Piquet's mood at the post-race press

> Despite all the Mansell mania of another home win, few observers could have failed to notice Nelson Piquet's mood at the post-race press conference.

conference. He sat alongside Mansell, totally exhausted and staring blankly into the middle distance. The body language said it all; he was finished with Williams, come hell or high water. Within another month he confirmed that he would be leaving the team to drive for the Lotus-Honda squad in 1988. Even so, he departed with the 1987 Drivers' World Championship.

In turn, Lotus team leader Ayrton Senna would join Alain Prost in the McLaren line-up. Using Honda engines transferred from Williams by the equally disillusioned Japanese car maker. Mansell stayed on with Williams for another season, during which the team struggled with uncompetitive Judd V10 engines. Then he left to join Ferrari, only to come back into the Williams fold for 1991.

That year, Nelson Piquet would be driving for the Benetton-Ford team. The Brazilian scored the last victory of his distinguished Formula 1 career in the Canadian Grand Prix at Montreal. He inherited it on the last lap when Mansell's Williams rolled to a halt barely a mile from the chequered flag. Needless to say, Piquet relished the irony. He and Mansell still disliked each other with a passion after all those years.

Reflecting on his time at Williams with Mansell, Piquet would say: "I didn't come into this team to compete with another driver. I had a contract as number one driver and they screwed up the whole thing."

"Technically they were the best team I worked with, but I didn't join them to apply my experience to setting up cars for a team-mate who then made it difficult for me to win races."

As at Adelaide the previous autumn, the intervention of the Goodyear tyre technicians played a central role in the outcome of the race.

Piquet leads Mansell and Senna's Lotus-Honda on the opening lap of the momentous 1987 British GP. But Nigel would turn the tables once again.

8 prost and senna

world
war III

The relationship between Alain Prost and Ayrton Senna promised to be difficult from the outset. Way back in 1984, when the Monaco Grand Prix was flagged to a halt at half distance in torrential rain, Prost only just shaved home the winner. His McLaren crossed the line a few lengths ahead of Senna's Toleman-Hart, the Brazilian proving the absolute sensation of the race and laying down a significant marker as to his future potential.

Previous page: Ayrton Senna shows a clean pair of heels to team-mate Alain Prost on the opening of the 1989 Monaco Grand Prix.

Right: The story of a season; the McLaren-Hondas of Senna and Prost running nose-to-tail in the 1988 French Grand Prix.

Ayrton Senna clinches his first World Championship at Suzuka, 1988. Prost (left) looks reflective.

At the start of 1985, two events occurred which convinced Prost that he should keep a firm eye out for Senna. The first took place at a press conference hosted by Marlboro, McLaren's main sponsor, immediately before the Brazilian Grand Prix at Rio. Senna, who was now backed by the rival John Player cigarette brand, obviously had to be invited to this gathering prior to his home race, but he was provisionally seated on the outer edge of the circle.

Yet before the other drivers arrived, Senna juggled the labels in order to end up sitting next to Niki Lauda, then the reigning World Champion. As he later recounted, Prost made a mental note that "Senna is an arriviste."

Later that year, in the San Marino Grand Prix, Senna drove in an aggressively defensive manner whilst trying to prevent Prost's McLaren from taking the lead. In the end it didn't matter, because Senna's Renault V6-engined Lotus ran out of fuel with three laps left to run and Prost took an easy victory – only to be disqualified when his car was found to be about one kilogramme beneath the 540kg minimum weight limit.

Early in his career, Senna gained a well-justified reputation as being technically astute when it came to F1 engine development. Just as Prost had developed a great skill when it came to setting up a Grand Prix chassis to get the best performance out of it across a race distance, so Senna seemed uniquely sensitive to engines. In theory, each of these qualities should have complemented the other when Ayrton joined Alain in the McLaren-Honda line-up for 1988. But things just did not unfold in such a predictable fashion.

Senna was not coming into the McLaren enclave

Prost heads for his 40th career victory in the 1990 French GP at the wheel of the Ferrari 642.

simply to be a team man. He was out to beat Prost hollow and establish himself as the best driver in the world. In pursuing this aim he would be immeasurably assisted by the fact that the 1988 McLaren-Honda MP4/4 turbo was head and shoulders above the opposition in terms of performance. It was really just a question of which McLaren would win which race.

At the end of the season, Senna won his first World Championship title with eight wins to Prost's seven. The Frenchman had found himself suffering in much the same way as Niki Lauda had done at his hands in 1984. Prost was now the seasoned campaigner, unwilling to put everything on the line for a kamikaze qualifying lap, dodging through gaps in traffic that might close before you got to them. He figured he could match Senna on racecraft and tactics, but not for sheer speed in qualifying.

Although their first season together in the

> At the end of the opening lap, Alain swooped out of Ayrton's slipstream at 170mph as they came past the pits, only for the Brazilian to swing left and edge Prost in towards the pit wall.

Ayrton Senna dominating the 1988 Detroit GP, as he did eight of the 16 races that season for McLaren.

McLaren team passed more or less without incident, it was certainly far from personally harmonious. Prost found competing with Senna stressful in the extreme. Ayrton seemed to thrive on tension and confrontation as a means of polishing his competitive edge. But at the 1988 Portuguese Grand Prix things very nearly became physical between the two McLaren drivers.

For some reason, Senna got it into his head that Prost had squeezed him out on the sprint to the first corner, although subsequent examination of television tapes revealed that this was certainly not the case. The race was stopped due to an accident amongst some of the tail-enders, after which Senna led the restart with Prost right on his tail.

At the end of the opening lap, Alain swooped out of Ayrton's slipstream at 170mph as they came past the pits, only for the Brazilian to swing left and edge Prost in towards the pit wall. Alain kept his foot

hard on the throttle and completed the manoeuvre. But strong words were exchanged in the motorhome after the race.

Into the 1989 season and the McLarens were now powered by non-turbo 3.5-litre V10 engines. These machines were still highly competitive, if not quite as dominantly so as the previous year. At the San Marino Grand Prix Senna and Prost qualified together on the front row of the starting grid and Ayrton suggested that they should agree to an informal 'no overtaking' rule on the first lap to prevent any unnecessary incident as they attempted to pull clear of the field.

Senna got away cleanly at the start, but the race was red-flagged to a halt following a major accident to Gerhard Berger's Ferrari on the seventh lap. At the restart, Prost got the jump on Senna, but Ayrton ducked past going into the Tosa hairpin on the opening lap, apparently breaching their tactic

arrangement. Prost was fit to be tied, but Ayrton lamely explained it away by reminding Alain that this was the restart – not the start.

This was really splitting hairs and McLaren boss Ron Dennis sat the two men down at a test session before the next race at Monaco. Ayrton was effectively railroaded into offering Prost an apology and

Senna's challenge in the 1990 Mexican GP was thwarted by a rear tyre failure.

When the talking had to stop. The McLarens of Senna and Prost after their collision whilst battling for the lead of the 1989 Japanese GP.

Dennis added: "In future, I will be part of any plan or arrangement the drivers might make."

In the aftermath of this episode, Prost began to toy with the idea of stopping racing there and then. He was angry with Senna beyond words, but remembered only too vividly how Villeneuve had been in the fortnight before his death after being duped by Pironi at Imola seven years earlier. Alain vowed that he was not going to risk a fatal accident by allowing emotion to get the better of him. On quiet reflection, he realised that Senna had pulled the wool over his eyes in precisely the same way Pironi had sought to do with Gilles. But he was not going to take the bait.

Despite suspicions that some Honda engines were more equal than others in terms of performance, Prost emerged from the British Grand Prix at mid-season with a commanding 20-point championship lead. Yet he was confused and uncertain. Senna had undermined his position at McLaren to such an extent that he found himself unable to commit to staying with the team in 1990 when Ron Dennis made him a formal offer. His morale had

been sapped and Ayrton had driven him out of his spiritual home. He would drive for Ferrari the following season, against the McLaren-Hondas.

Yet there was much more trouble to come. In qualifying for the Japanese Grand Prix at Suzuka, Senna may have taken pole position by more than a second from Prost, but it was all different come the race. At the last moment before the start, Alain gambled on reducing aerodynamic downforce on his car to squeeze out a fraction more straight-line speed. At the start, he launched himself straight into the lead from second place on the front row of the grid.

What followed was an epic Grand Prix battle between two of the sport's leading exponents. Senna pulled every trick in the book to get on terms with his team-mate, seemingly to no avail. But Senna would not ease up. With six laps left, he made a superhuman effort, slamming through the fast left-hander before the pit chicane only inches away from Prost's rear wing. He then pulled out and made to outbrake the Frenchman into the chicane.

Prost reckoned that Senna was now relying on his good grace to make room for him to complete the overtaking manoeuvre. But Alain was fed up with two years of intimidation at the hands of the Brazilian and closed the door. The two McLaren-Hondas slithered to a halt, locked together in the middle of the circuit. It was a farcical situation.

Prost undid his belts and climbed from the cockpit, convinced that the World Championship battle was now resolved in his favour. Ayrton, however, beckoned to the marshals to push-start his car. But he then resumed the race by proceeding through the chicane escape road, rather than back-tracking on to the circuit itself. In so doing, he gave officialdom a stick with which to beat him.

In qualifying for the Japanese Grand Prix at Suzuka, Senna may have taken pole position by more than a second from Prost, but it was all different come the race.

Senna at speed in Brazil, 1989, one race he didn't manage to win.

Ayrton recovered to win ahead of Alessandro Nannini's Benetton, but was excluded for not going through the chicane properly. McLaren appealed the sentence at an FIA court of appeal which met the following Friday, where they were taken aback to be presented with a savage indictment of Senna's aggressive driving style. Eventually the exclusion was upheld, together with a $100,000 fine and a six-month suspended driving ban. Senna and McLaren were absolutely outraged and Ayrton, believing that Prost was the arch-demon in all this, resolutely decided to have nothing more to do with the French driver.

Senna spent the following winter in his native Brazil, convinced that Jean-Marie Balestre, the President of the FIA, had manipulated the championship in Prost's favour. He even considered retiring from the sport, but eventually climbed down, withdrew his allegations and paid his fine. But of course that did nothing to mollify his continuing hatred of Prost, who in 1990 would be facing him from the cockpit of a Ferrari.

Despite attempts at a rapprochement at Monza, prompted by a journalist who asked them whether it was not time to end the feud, Senna was still clearly consumed by the previous year's events at Suzuka and was simply not prepared to let the matter rest. On the return to the Japanese track, Senna again complained that, as it had been the previous year, pole position was off-line on the dusty right-hand side of the circuit. He wanted it changed, so the fastest qualifier – him – could start on the clean left-hand side of the track. Agreement to this change was not forthcoming.

On race morning, Senna hinted that Prost – who had qualified second in his Ferrari – had better watch out. "If he gets to the first corner ahead of me, he'd better not turn in because he's not going to make it," he threatened. And so events unfolded. Prost's Ferrari accelerated cleanly away into the lead, but Ayrton simply didn't brake and rammed him off the track going into the first right-hander. Both cars were out of the race and Senna was champion for the second time.

End of the road. Senna's McLaren and Prost's Ferrari after their first corner collision at Suzuka in 1990.

Left: Prost is now in a Ferrari (No 1), but Senna's McLaren is still in command as the pack sprints for the first corner of the 1990 Monaco Grand Prix.

On race morning, Senna hinted that Prost – who had qualified second in his Ferrari – had better watch out.

"The World Championship is won over a full season, not at an individual race," said Senna flatly, by way of explanation. It was a state of affairs that defied belief, particularly in view of the fact that neither the race stewards nor the sport's governing body imposed any sanction against Senna. This time the incident was shrugged aside as no more than a racing accident.

Through 1991 the rivalry continued, but Prost took a sabbatical in 1992 and chose not to race. In 1993, however, he returned to take over Nigel Mansell's place as team leader in the Williams-Renault squad, where he specifically excluded Senna from being recruited as a possible partner. Ayrton felt this was a totally unacceptable way in which to behave, accusing Prost of being cowardly, wanting to monopolize the best car and so on. The Brazilian's frustration was heightened by the fact that McLaren had lost its Honda works engine contract and was now having to pay for Cosworth Ford V8 power units.

Ayrton initially only drove for the team on a race-to-race basis, but eventually completed the entire season to score five wins at the wheel of the McLaren-Ford. But Prost won the championship – only to be ousted from Williams for 1994 by his arch-rival. On the face of it, Senna had won the final battle with Prost and the Frenchman was now retiring for good with his fourth title crown.

For the 1994 San Marino Grand Prix, Prost arrived at the Imola circuit in his new role as commentator for French television. Strangely, in view of what had gone before, Ayrton made time to talk to him at some length. There were signs of a genuine healing of old wounds between the two men for what was really the first time since the height of their on-track feuding. Prost thought Senna had become less intense, perhaps realising that there was more in life than simply Grand Prix racing.

Yet the process of reconciliation between the two men was destined to go no further. Senna was killed on race day at Imola, crashing at high speed while leading in his Williams-Renault. Five days later Prost would be amongst the pallbearers at Senna's funeral in Sao Paulo. One of the most fraught, complex and emotional chapters in Grand Prix racing history had abruptly come to an end.

Senna's McLaren leads Prost's Ferrari in the early stages of the 1990 Spanish GP at Jerez.

9 hill and schumacher

magnetic attraction

In the media-driven Formula 1 environment of the 1990s, it was hardly surprising that the rivalry between Damon Hill and Michael Schumacher attracted such prominent billing. In many ways, it was the tabloid's dream story. The determined young son of Britain's great Grand Prix hero of yesterday taking on the clean-cut German superstar. It had all the elements of a sure-fire box office success.

ronically, although the Hill/Schumacher saga would develop an extremely unpleasant edge, neither of the participants originally went out looking for trouble. The death of Ayrton Senna in the 1994 San Marino Grand Prix had a far-reaching effect on both men. Schumacher stepped forward as the logical claimant to Senna's position as the leading F1 driver of the moment, while Hill, left behind to pick up the pieces as the Williams team's lead driver, had to do his best to occupy the void left by the dynamic Brazilian.

In fact, the first serious wheel-to-wheel confrontation between the two men actually occurred at Imola on the afternoon of Senna's death. In the restarted race, Damon lost a nose wing against one of Schumacher's rear wheels as they jostled for position early on in the contest. Schumacher won for Benetton; Damon finished sixth, after a delay to fit a replacement nose section, and gained fastest lap as some consolation.

Making hay in Schumacher's absence; Hill wins at Monza, 1994.

In the aftermath of Senna's death, although Hill took a lucky win in the Spanish Grand Prix, it took him a couple of races to find his competitive feet, yet by the French GP at Magny-Cours he was certainly emerging as Schumacher's most consistent challenger. In the following race, the British Grand Prix at Silverstone, Hill won commandingly after Schumacher had been penalized with a 10 second stop-go penalty for getting out of position on the parade lap immediately prior to the start.

Worse still, the Benetton team management prevaricated with the stewards, causing Schumacher to ignore the black flag for a couple of laps before coming in to take the penalty concerned. An inquiry was immediately initiated by the World Motor Sport Council and Schumacher was given a two-race ban and disqualified from second place at Silverstone, and the Benetton team fined $500,000.

By any standards, these were swingeing penalties which, in the view of many observers, tended to signal that the FIA felt there were aspects of the Benetton B194's technical eligibility which were not all they might be – even though the team was officially given a clean bill of health on this point later in the season. But it immediately triggered wild

Hill tails Schumacher early in the rain-soaked 1994 Japanese GP, which Damon went through to win in brilliant style to keep open his title hopes.

Adelaide, 1994; the nose of Schumacher's Benetton after it had speared into a tyre barrier and out of the race.

Right: Before the hugging had to stop. Hill and Schumacher after Michael's victory over the Englishman in the 1994 Hungarian GP.

Schumacher was in a class of his own at Hungary in 1994, convincingly beating Hill's Williams into second place.

suspicions in Schumacher's mind that the sport's governing body was attempting to 'fix' the outcome of the championship to favour his rival.

This view was heightened when Schumacher found himself disqualified from victory in the Belgian Grand Prix at Spa for another technical infringement. Hill inherited the victory, then went on to win the Italian Grand Prix at Monza and the Portuguese race at Estoril while Schumacher stayed at home, twiddling his thumbs and sitting out his two-race suspension.

Just before his return to the championship stage for the Grand Prix of Europe at Jerez, Schumacher made some pointed observations to the effect that Damon was nothing more than a second-class contender. On the face of it, these simply looked like foolishly intemperate remarks, but, in retrospect, it seems that Michael was deliberately attempting to undermine Hill's position as they went into the final few races of the season.

Damon remained stoically unimpressed, describing Schumacher's observations as "a pretty half-baked effort to try and destabilize me, but he'll have to do rather better than that."

"I would rather not drag the championship down in that way by trying to diminish the reputation of the opposition. I think it is sad that, for too long, Formula 1 has got itself into the situation where the two leading protagonists seemingly hate each other's guts."

"I think it is bad for the sport, bad for F1 and especially so in a season when we've lost a great champion in Ayrton Senna. I would prefer a clean, sporting fight for the last three races. I think Michael's remarks are ill-conceived and immature."

Nevertheless, although Hill led the Jerez race

during its opening stages, he was eventually defeated by Schumacher after a slight glitch with the Williams team's refuelling equipment. With two races left to run, Schumacher had 86 points and Hill 81. But then Schumacher had the fright of his life when Hill beat him in a straight fight to win the rain-soaked Japanese Grand Prix at Suzuka.

"This is the first time that Michael has been beaten fair and square all season," admitted Damon. "I put myself under a lot of pressure and, for that reason, I think this win is even more satisfying than the one I scored at Silverstone."

Ironically, Hill chose this moment to pile even more pressure on himself, on the eve of the season's finale in Australia at a time when he was trailing Schumacher by only a single point. It was, he felt, the moment to address what he believed was the Williams team's obvious lack of faith in his ability.

Put simply, he did not believe he was being paid enough and this lack of financial recompense could be interpreted as reflecting the team's fundamental indifference towards him.

His irritation was compounded by the fact that Renault, the Williams team's engine suppliers, had expressed a preference for Nigel Mansell's presence in the team for 1995. "I am pretty disgusted with some of the things that have gone on," said Damon firmly on his arrival in Adelaide. "I feel that they

**Putting a brave face on it;
Hill and Schumacher, 1994.**

**Hill's lowest moment:
Monaco, 1994, where he was
eliminated in a first lap
shunt.**

Hill leads the opening lap at Budapest from Coulthard and Schumacher en route to a fine victory in the 1995 Hungarian GP.

Hill starts 1995 on a promising note, winning the second round of the championship in Argentina.

have not contributed to making me feel that the team is behind me to win the championship.

"I have been in negotiation with the team about my contract. They have taken up their option on my services for next year, but I reckon I am a lot better than my contract says I am. The dispute is about the team recognising what you feel yourself to be worth."

Come the race, Damon did everything and more to dispel speculation over his value. After only managing to qualify third behind Mansell's Williams and Schumacher, he pulled up on to the Benetton's tail after only a handful of laps and began to apply relentless pressure to his young German rival.

They battled it out head to head for 36 laps before Michael made a mistake, slid off the circuit and glanced a wall with his Benetton's right rear tyre.

Hill at this point had dropped several lengths behind and was back around the previous corner at the moment of Schumacher's impact; he only saw the Benetton coming back on to the track off the grass. But Damon judged that he had to go for it,

diving for the inside of the Benetton as they went into the next right-hander.

But Schumacher cut back across and, in a trice, his Benetton vaulted over the Williams's left front wheel, crashed down and went sliding into a tyre barrier. Hill was left to limp slowly back to the pits, but his car was damaged beyond repair. Schumacher had won the World Championship by the margin of a single point.

Damon had given his all and gone down to defeat with dignity. Amidst the post-race euphoria, Schumacher seemed to acknowledge this and went some way to make amends for suggesting that Hill was a second-rate driver. "I have to admit I was wrong," he said. "He has been a great rival and I must say sorry for what I maybe have said." Hill thus finished an emotionally trying season with his head held high. But his rivalry with Michael Schumacher was nowhere near finished, as the 1995 season would prove.

The new F1 season kicked off with Williams clearly having the best car, but Damon and his team-mate David Coulthard were hit by a frustrating degree of mechanical unreliability. Hill briefly led the championship points table with two wins out of the first three races, but then wilted as Schumacher's title defence gained momentum.

Their first clash came in the French Grand Prix,

Hill was left to limp slowly back to the pits, but his car was damaged beyond repair. Schumacher was World Champion by the margin of a single point.

where Hill led the early stages and Schumacher accused him of 'brake testing' his Benetton as they came up to lap a slower car early in the race. Hill shrugged aside the allegations, but then put his own driving skill under the spotlight of critical scrutiny when he collided with Schumacher as they battled for the lead of the British Grand Prix at Silverstone.

A multiple collision at the first corner caused the 1994 Italian GP to be stopped, but Hill (No 0, foreground) won the Monza restart.

While Damon attempted to explain away the incident as nothing more than a racing accident, Schumacher got really stuck into his rival. "It was completely unnecessary what Damon did there," he claimed. "There was no room and he came from nowhere. I don't see the sense of doing things like this, even in front of your home crowd. You have to keep your nerve and temperament and not be a danger to anyone. It's more or less the same situation as Adelaide, where he tried to dive inside and

Hill thus finished an emotionally trying season with his head held high. But his rivalry with Michael Schumacher was nowhere near finished, as the 1995 season would prove.

there was no room. I can't understand it. Damon was probably under too much pressure and tried to do something that wouldn't work."

Schumacher's tentative bracketing of the Silverstone and Adelaide incidents was cheeky by any standards, for many F1 insiders regarded the German driver as solely responsible for the collision which resolved the outcome of the 1994 World

Championship. However, on a day when Frank Williams was widely rumoured to have described Damon as 'a prat', Schumacher clearly decided to press home his psychological advantage.

Hill then played straight into his hands by spinning off the road on the second lap of the German Grand Prix at Hockenheim. He regained his composure to score a decisive victory in the Hungarian Grand Prix, where Schumacher failed to finish, but from then on Damon was very definitely on the run. Schumacher now had the upper hand and slammed home his advantage to build up an increasingly impregnable points lead as the European season approached its end.

Schumacher and Hill banged wheels during their battle in the Belgian Grand Prix at Spa, prompting Damon to ask for a clarification as to just what was and was not permitted in terms of tactics when driving in close company. Unfortunately he followed this up by ramming Michael off the track at Monza

Damon's 1995 British GP foray ended in disappointment when he tangled with Schumacher and both went off.

Seconds before contact. Schumacher's Benetton (right) is about to brush wheels with Hill's Williams as they battle for the lead of the 1995 Belgian GP at Spa.

Schumacher prepares for action at the start of the 1994 Canadian GP in his Benetton-Ford B194.

during the Italian Grand Prix. He received a one-race suspended ban for this performance, prompting an indignant response from Schumacher, who had been rewarded for his Spa performance with a similar penalty – but suspended for four races rather than for one race, which Damon received at Spa.

If Hill was to have a hope of salvaging his title challenge, he had to win the Portuguese Grand Prix at Estoril. No chance. His team-mate David Coulthard stormed to a convincing maiden F1 victory from pole position, leaving Damon trailing

Schumacher at the chequered flag. He was now 17 points down with four races – and 40 points – left to fight for.

Schumacher then won again in front of his home crowd at the Nurburgring, producing one of his best ever drives in the European Grand Prix. Hill crashed. Now the Englishman was 27 points down with three races to run and effectively conceded the championship. Finally, Schumacher conclusively clinched his second title with a convincing victory in the Pacific Grand Prix at Aida with Coulthard

As if this wasn't enough, Schumacher told Hill that he wasn't happy with his driving tactics in the early part of the race. Damon at least managed to use this as a means of getting back at his rival in a week when the FIA had effectively decred that 'anything goes' as long as it could not be construed as being deliberately dangerous.

"I find this completely extraordinary," said Hill. "The situation now is that we are completely free to drive as we like as long as it is not deliberately dangerous. So I drove in that style and he did not like it. He should have no complaints. It seems that there is one rule for him and another for everybody else."

If life is all about little victories, then Hill could at least console himself with evening the account, albeit only fractionally, with this rejoinder. Even Schumacher later acknowledged that he had watched a video tape of the incident and that Damon, after all, was not to blame.

By then, of course, it was too late. Schumacher had gone on to win the Japanese Grand Prix at Suzuka, his ninth victory of the season. Hill was left trailing with three. As far as the 1995 World Championship contest was concerned, Damon was on the canvas.

The big question mark was now whether he could pick himself up, dust himself down and square up to Schumacher in 1996 as if none of this unpleasantness had ever taken place.

and Hill trailing home in second and third place for the Williams team.

Going into the Pacific GP, Schumacher continued his attempts to psychologically bury Hill. "Damon's biggest problem is that he doesn't appear to be in control when he is trying to overtake. He makes half-hearted attempts which land him in trouble – with no way out." These remarks were aggravated by a chorus of disapproval from fellow F1 competitors Coulthard and Martin Brundle, all of which took their toll on Damon's resilience.

Hill's Williams leads into the first corner of the 1994 British GP at Silverstone with Schumacher heading the pursuit.

head
to head

When Jacques Villeneuve bounced on to the Formula 1 scene at the start of the 1996 World Championship season, most experienced observers were more than a little sceptical. Granted, he had a famous name. Son of the legendary Ferrari ace Gilles Villeneuve, killed during practice for the 1982 Belgian Grand Prix, this young French-Canadian had made his own mark on the international motor racing scene, stamping his achievements in North America with his own very personal trademark.

In 1995 Villeneuve won the Indianapolis 500, America's most famous motor race, and continued to win the Indycar championship. Yet now he wanted to try his hand at Formula 1. It seemed like a long shot, but there was one influential man who was very keen on the whole exercise.

Bernie Ecclestone, the multi-millionaire vice president of motor racing's governing body, the FIA, concluded that Villeneuve would be an asset to the F1 scene. He would possibly raise television viewer interest in the United States at a time when Formula 1 was trying to re-establish itself there. And poaching the top Indycar runner from the rival US domestic racing series would be something of a personal coup for Grand Prix racing as a whole.

Ecclestone persuaded Frank Williams, owner of Britain's top Formula 1 team in the 1990s, to consider the plan. After a couple of test sessions, Williams duly signed up Villeneuve for the 1996 season. By any standards, it would turn out to be a dynamically imaginative decision.

On his first Grand Prix outing, Villeneuve simply dazzled the opposition. He qualified on pole position ahead of his team-mate Damon Hill and, had it not been for an oil leak late in the race, he might well have won on his maiden outing. As it was, Jacques finished a very creditable second.

The 1996 championship battle turned into a head-to-head with Damon Hill, who only took the title by winning the very last Grand Prix race of the season in Japan. Yet as the season wore on, it became increasingly clear that Villeneuve was emerging as one of the great new talents on the F1 horizon. Thus, it was almost preordained that he should eventually find himself pitched into a head-to-head confrontation with Michael Schumacher, the driver regarded as the most gifted performer in the Grand Prix firmament.

Seconds to go before the start of the 1997 European Grand Prix at Jerez. Villeneuve (foreground) is on pole position, but Schumacher's Ferrari (top) will make the better start.

At the start of the 1996 season, Schumacher had moved from Benetton to Williams. With a handsome $25 million retainer from the famous Italian team, his avowed intention was to help build Ferrari back up to the point where it could win its first drivers' championship crown since 1979.

The German driver had already won the championship in 1994 and 95. Hailed as being the greatest F1 talent to emerge since Ayrton Senna, he duly consolidated that mantle after the legendary Brazilian was killed in the 1994 San Marino Grand Prix at Imola. Nothing, it seemed, could now prevent Schumacher from breaking all the records in the history books.

Yet in only the fourth race of the 1996 season, Schumacher had a worrying taste of what he could expect from Villeneuve. The Canadian performed brilliantly under the most daunting pressure imaginable to cross the line first in the European Grand Prix at the Nurburgring, winning a scant 0.7 second ahead of the reigning champion Schumacher's Ferrari, which had tailed him relentlessly for half the 67-lap race waiting for the slip that never came.

It was a success that consolidated Jacques' second place in the World Championship points table, only 11 behind title leader Damon Hill, who battled hard after a poor start from pole position and could count himself fortunate to finish fourth, having slipped as low as 11th at one point during the early stages of the race.

In winning on only his fourth Grand Prix outing, Villeneuve matched the achievement of the legendary Brazilian ace Emerson Fittipaldi, who achieved the same feat for Lotus in the 1970 United States GP. Only the late Giancarlo Baghetti, who won the 1961 French GP on his maiden outing, had bettered this achievement.

"It's a great feeling to win my first race in F1," he said, "and it's great for the whole team as well, because we've been competitive since the beginning of the season and finally we get it on the highest step of the podium. It's great, because we've worked hard to get there."

It was understandable that Villeneuve should make the odd slip during his first F1 season, but he certainly did enough for Schumacher to note that here was somebody he could not underestimate.

On his first visit to the spectacularly fast Spa-Francorchamps circuit for the 1996 Belgian Grand Prix, Villeneuve finished a strong second behind Schumacher's Ferrari. Then, during the Portuguese Grand Prix, Villeneuve overtook Schumacher *round*

Ferrari versus Williams. Schumacher's Ferrari (leading) was technically not quite a match for Villeneuve's Williams in 1997, but Michael's brilliant driving talent made up the difference.

the outside of the flat-out right-hand corner before the pits. Michael smiled approvingly when questioned on this at the post-race media conference.

However, it would not take long for this indulgent attitude to undergo a radical change. If in 1996 Schumacher had regarded Villeneuve as something of an amusing newcomer, in 1997 he found himself pitched head-to-head with the Canadian in a battle for the World Championship.

Villeneuve began the season strongly, winning the Brazilian and Argentine Grands Prix to establish an early championship lead. But then Schumacher won at Monaco and Canada – where Jacques suffered the humiliation of spinning off in front of his home crowd – and then again in France.

Villeneuve, who had managed an impressive victory in the Spanish Grand Prix, then added the British race to his list of victories before his form suddenly wobbled quite dramatically. He was lucky to win the Hungarian Grand Prix, then Schumacher triumphed brilliantly in Belgium for the second year running and it began to seem as though the title battle would go right down to the wire.

The biggest controversy came in the Japanese Grand Prix, where Villeneuve was excluded from the race after allegedly failing to slow down when the yellow warning flags were displayed during a practice session. The Williams team appealed against this penalty, so Jacques was permitted to start the race. Having qualified on pole position, he accelerated into an immediate lead and drove deliberately slowly in order to keep the following pack boxed in tightly behind him.

With Schumacher in second place, Jacques might have been forgiven for thinking that an exuberant rival would make a bid to overtake the Ferrari and knock off his rival – innocently, of course. In the event, Schumacher went on to win, thanks in part to some questionable assistance from team-mate Eddie Irvine. Villeneuve finally finished fifth, ostensibly facing the final round of the World Championship just one point ahead of Schumacher.

Yet the FIA court of appeal duly rejected the Williams team's appeal and Jacques was disqualified, losing the two points that accrued for fifth place. Now he was one point behind Schumacher going into the last race of the season, the European Grand Prix at Jerez, southern Spain.

The two title rivals went to the starting line amid a mood of enormous tension and expectancy. Villeneuve's pole position was on the cleaner left-hand side of the circuit, but many people predicted that Schumacher was more favourably placed on the right-hand side of the track, aiming for the first right hander. And so it proved.

"I wasn't on new tyres from the start of the race and I had to struggle to keep up with Michael," said Villeneuve. "At the start he was glued to the asphalt, I don't know how he did it. I was impressed, because I was sliding everywhere. Then he was on the inside of me going into the first corner after the start and my team-mate Heinz-Harald Frentzen

The photo which was beamed around the world. Michael Schumacher's Ferrari (left) slams the door on Jacques Villeneuve's Williams in the 1997 European Grand Prix at Jerez. It resolved the outcome of the title battle in the Canadian driver's favour.

came up on the inside of me and I gave him room because I didn't want to risk banging wheels with him at this early stage in the race."

By the end of the opening lap, Schumacher was 1.9 seconds ahead of Frentzen, with Villeneuve third from the McLaren-Mercedes of Mika Hakkinen and David Coulthard. It took until lap eight before Jacques went ahead of his team-mate to take second place, after which the Williams team leader immediately steadied the Ferrari's advantage at 4.2 seconds, fading slightly to 4.7 seconds by lap 12.

On lap 22 Schumacher tension was heightened as he made his first refuelling stop in 7.6 seconds, resuming fourth behind Villeneuve, Frentzen and Hakkinen. Now the race became acutely tactical. On lap 23 Villeneuve made his first refuelling stop, dropping down the order to fifth behind Coulthard.

On lap 25 Coulthard obligingly pulled in from fourth place to make his first refuelling stop, which allowed Villeneuve to pull up on to Schumacher's Ferrari. On lap 26 Hakkinen made his first stop, then Frentzen headed for the pit lane on lap 28 and, hey presto, Schumacher and Villeneuve were back in first and second places separated by only 0.9 second.

Since his first stop, Villeneuve had been on fresh rubber and was now piling on the pressure. From 3.1 seconds behind, the gap came down to 2.0 seconds on lap 35, then 1.7 seconds on lap 40. Ralf Schumacher, running the spare Jordan, did his bit

(Above) Ignominious end. Schumacher's Ferrari F310B is hoisted onto a recovery truck after the German driver's collision with Villeneuve at Jerez which resolved the destiny of the 1997 World Championship. (Left) A stern-faced Schumacher gets a lift back to the pits.

to help big brother as they lapped the Peugeot-engined car on lap 40, but it cost Villeneuve only 0.4 second.

Schumacher made his second refuelling stop at the end of lap 43, followed by Villeneuve a lap later. Again the Williams driver got back into the race third behind Coulthard, but again the McLaren driver cleared the way by coming in for his stop next time around.

Now Villeneuve was all over Schumacher's rear wing and lunged for the inside going into Dry Sack, the sixth corner. Then, the two cars collided.

"I knew I had to make my move then, or else my tyres would go off a bit and I wouldn't be able to fight anymore," said Villeneuve. "I just went for it, and just braked late. I was surprised that he hadn't closed the door yet, but it was only a matter of seconds before he decided to turn in on me. But he did not do it well enough – he went out and I didn't. The impact was very hard. The way we banged wheels was hard enough to break my suspension. It was not a small thing, but the car felt strange and I took the next few laps pretty slowly. Once I was sure that the suspension was not touching the tyre I managed to press on intermittently . . ."

Villeneuve at speed in the Williams-Renault FW19. Despite a slight mid-season slump, the Canadian bounced back to finish 1997 strongly and suceed Damon Hill as World Champion.

Schumacher's Ferrari was beached in the gravel trap, along with its driver's World Championship hopes. Despite concerns that his car had sustained quite serious damage, Villeneuve was left to battle poor handling and unpredictable tyre wear for the remainder of the distance, before easing his pace on the final lap to allow Mika Hakkinen and David Coulthard through to score a McLaren-Mercedes 1–2 as a "thank you" for the apparent tacit help they had given him earlier in the race.

After the race both Schumacher and Villeneuve were summoned to the stewards to explain the collision. It was decided that this was a racing accident, but 24 hours later – after Schumacher reaped a whirlwind of vitriolic criticism, particularly from the Italian and German media – the FIA stepped in to summon the Ferrari driver to appear before an extraordinary meeting of its World Council.

Despite pre-race warnings from senior officials that the final round of the championship should be free of such aggressive confrontations, it was decided that Schumacher had turned into the Williams's left-hand side pod as the Canadian driver dived through on the inside to take the lead. It was widely perceived as a rerun of the controversial accident

with Damon Hill at Adelaide in 1994, which Schumacher has since consistently denied was a deliberate attempt to force his rival off the track.

Unlike 1994, this time Schumacher came off second best and paid an even heavier price when the FIA disqualified him from second place in the World Championship points table. Many observers thought that the German driver had got off quite lightly under the circumstances.

Schumacher was rocked by the FIA's decision. Up until then, the German *wunderkind* had seemingly led a charmed life as a member of Grand Prix motor racing's elite. Now he had not only been beaten by a relative newcomer, but his own behaviour had been judged by the sport's rulers to be seriously lacking.

Michael tried to brush it aside by saying that, after all, they'd been out for a beer together on the evening after the race. Things couldn't be that bad.

Yet Villeneuve saw it differently. "We're not close friends, nor ever will be," he insisted. "All this stuff about us being close is just rubbish. It's not true. Michael is a good driver, but he's certainly not unbeatable. And I believe that I can continue to beat him in 1998."

Everything had changed. Now there was talk that the new World Champion was poised to move his career up a notch. No longer just the blond kid in the best car, shaking a stick at Michael Schumacher. Suddenly he had become the man who might – just might – have the nerve to topple the Ferrari driver from his perceived position atop the F1 pile.

Patrick Head, the Williams team's technical director put it succinctly. "Jacques is very confident and controlled. The general view is that he's a very good driver, but not in Michael Schumacher's class. He wants to put that right. He wants to show either that he is in Schumacher's class or better."

As the 1998 World Championship season was poised to begin, many F1 observers believed that Jacques Villeneuve had done that already.

Jacques Villeneuve is carried aloft by his fans in the pit at Jerez after clinching the 1997 World Championship with a controversial third place in the European Grand Prix.

First published in 1996 by

George Weidenfeld & Nicolson Limited

This edition published in 1998 by

Phoenix Illustrated,

The Orion Publishing Group

Orion House

5 Upper St. Martin's Lane

London WC2H 9EA

British Library Cataloguing-in-Publication Data

A catalogue record for this book is available

from the British Library.

ISBN 0-75380-522-7

Designed by The Design Revolution, Brighton